Joshua Adler

PHILOSOPHY
OF
JUDAISM

THE PHILOSOPHICAL LIBRARY
New York

CONTENTS

PROLOGUE

It is not without reluctance that I commence this task. The task is a very nebulous one at best, and the path that leads to the ill-perceived goal is strewn with many obstacles. It is inconceivable that I should, therefore, start out on the journey without attempting some justification to my audience and to my own person for this action of divulging my ideas in writing. It is even more necessary since I am a person of very limited ability and my writing skill is one of my weakest assets, as you shall shortly no doubt perceive.

It might sound naive for me to say that the chief motivating cause for this undertaking is that the topic of this book has become rather fashionable of late. At least this is the reason for my unveiling it into the light of public scrutiny. It is in an attempt to give in print some ideas which are counter to present day popular fashionable religious thought that I at all succumb to fashion. You may have need for me to identify what the topic we shall be discussing is; I shall inform you that it is *universal religion.* Universal religion is nothing more nor less than the intellectual activity concerning the tenets of various religions and religious institutions; a complementary phenomenon to the more easily observable sacramental participation in these religions. I need not qualify my stating that both of these aspects of religious practice are now on the increase, and in the general terminology of America, fashionable.

This religious intellectual activity I call universal religion, since it is to find the *universal standard* of the particular ordinances of a religion that we think about this religion. If this statement is not sufficient for some, one must pardon me, since to explain universal religion is the task of this work. I hope that when you have been done going through the ideas herein stated, that this term as well as some other concepts I shall propose will not seem uncomfortable to you.

3

It is somewhat difficult for me to depict why I should now feel intuitively that I can transcend all of my human frailty. I can best arrive at communicating this intuition to you by using some analogies. The individual perceives of the universe as a huge puzzle. He is given all the parts to the puzzle, at least he thinks he has all the parts, and his objective is to fit these pieces together. The poorer individual picks up the first pieces that come to his hands and attempts a matching. He gropes about, usually matching a few pieces here and a few there, getting after much toil a few larger pieces instead of many smaller pieces. He may eventually terminate the puzzle thusly, but the work and time involved is great. The individual with more foresight perceives that the best method available to him in his job of fitting the parts together is to make the entire outside rim or frame first. Once the frame is set up he begins to work inwards towards the center until he has the complete picture. Both individuals do not feel entirely at ease until they have placed the last piece of the puzzle in place. Yet our second individual has two advantages over the first individual. First of all his method will lead him more feasibly to his goal, since the frame, once put together, gives us some idea of the position of the other pieces. And in the second place, once we have the frame together we have accomplished something. We have by no means solved the puzzle but we have in a sense solved part of it and if we were to stop here could not feel as if we had wasted our time. Our first fellow may deceive himself and think that he has accomplished, but we know better. A few large stones are not much better to us than a few smaller stones in our construction. With them we haven't even the key to our puzzle yet. With our frame we have certainly that key to the solution of the puzzle.

The pieces of the world puzzle may be infinite and the task of matching the pieces to get a panorama of the world may be eternal. Yet in the world puzzle as in the physical cardboard puzzle the need to build a frame first is apparent. This frame gives us the duplex accomplishment of being a guide for building inward or to the more specific, and as a plateau on which we can rest in our climb with a sense of satisfaction. This outline, in the world of ideas is well known and is called the *frame of reference*.

It is just such a frame of reference which I am attempting to outline in this work. I will attempt to add some pieces in the interior of the puzzle to help garnish my framework; yet my knowledge is terribly limited and thus the embellishment will be most rudimentary. I know that this will leave my work somewhat cold, incomplete and skeleton like. Yet I cannot help remarking that if we have a skeleton, we have the means of attaching the necessary organs in order to make it alive and vital, but if we are lacking the skeleton then the other organs shall be nought but a heap of crumples.

We must before further ado set the limits and the proportions of the task we are about to engage in. Our task is, of course, to answer a question. Weighing each word carefully, I will state the question as follows:

What is the unique Jewish experience, and Why?

In this manner I have been able to state four questions in one. You will no doubt see that I am asking what is the Jewish experience and what is its unique quality in juxtaposition to other extant religions. And for both of these variables I am asking that elusive monosyllabic word question of the mature mind, why?

In the progressive development towards maturity, the mind asks three distinct questions in its search towards comprehension of a problem which it encounters. The first question is the what question. It meets the strange entity and cannot grasp it at all until it has learned what it is. For certain minds and for certain problems no further quest is

5

necessary. For those entities which remain perplexed or perplexing the next attack that the mind has is how? Here the surface remarks of an object's existence and superficial remarks of its depiction will not suffice. A deeper understanding of the workings or mechanism, if you will, of the entity's existence is required. Once this is achieved and the subject can now be depicted in more detailed analysis, many more problems and people discontinue the search. However, there is a part of humanity, and one likes to think, a part of every mind, which encounters certain perplexing situations which no matter how much we can grasp the what and how of its existence, we will feel a void if we don't ask and find answer for the why of its existence. And the answer for the why question cannot be in terms of analysis inward of the problem but in analysis outward, namely in relating it to certain other entities. One must state before proceeding that the mere asking on any one level of questioning is no guarantee of obtaining an answer. Quite the contrary, that certain questions are destined to be unanswerable, is the truth.

It is almost unimaginable for a discussion of religious thought not to reach all three plateaus in the mind's probing operations, for religion itself is the realm of dealing with the why aspect of existence, in a certain method. It is safe to state, I think, that if religion were to make us feel satisfied concerning our existence in some intuitive form, it would be superfluous for us to ask, why religion? For it would be accomplishing its task and we would encounter no problem. It is precisely since we find that perhaps religion, any religion or our own religion, is not really answering or establishing the why of existence that we must ask why religion.

Why does one today find this sudden need to explain one's religion? Although all religions that I encounter are now issuing a rash of statements, in various media forms, to justify their presence, I find that Judaism is perhaps issuing the most statements, proportional to its size. I also surmise from the few items of this sort which I have undertaken to study that my religion is quite a bit in need of such reevaluating. And I attempt to state in a concise fashion why this is so.

Probably the single word-idea which gives us the method to deal with this issue is history. History has taken some quite gigantic leaps and bounds in the past several hundred years. It is also quite apparent, although at this moment no reason is suggested, that history seems to be quickening its pace, as of late. This duplex aspect of modern world history, its great deal of changed situations and its somewhat mystifying increase in pace, has left a heavier load of work on the shoulders of scholars and intellectuals. These people, whatever else they may do or not do, give us the terminology and the methods whereby we can explain phenomena. Now since phenomena have decided to increase themselves and also increase their rate of increasing, and since mental ability is still quite at a premium, the natural consequences of heavy working schedules for scholars is apparent.

This is true for general scholarship and doubly true for Jewish scholarship. For Jewish scholarship has, for reasons which I am not fully able to grasp, stopped interpreting itself to the world four centuries ago. Until that time each change in the intellectual makeup of general society forced upon the Jewish minority society within it to forge an interpretation, or if you wish a reconciliation, with the terminology and methods of the predominant intellectual current. This interpretation was not premeditated by the needs to explain ourselves to our neighbors, but by the needs to explain ourselves to ourselves. We have been able to keep the Torah only then when we were able to interpret it into the terminology and methods of the intellectual clime. Jews have been accused or admired for their ability to remain aloof from dominant social trends. This has been only half a truth. They have been thus able only then when their own tradition, no matter how incongruent with extant norms, has been in harmony with the dominant intellectual currents; this through the process of identification of its ideas and terminology with that of the intellectual currents. This is precisely what Maimonides accomplished in his *Guide to the Perplexed*. It was an interpretation of the axioms of Torah within the ideas of Aristotelian scholasticism. And it was an interpretation for Jews, since it made it possible for the Jew, at least for the learned Jew who felt the problem, to live with his tradition in the new clime of ideas.

Since the bursting of the so referred to medieval "city of G-d" in the sixteenth and seventeenth centuries, and the several distinct historical eras afterward which have been recorded for posterity, Jewish scholarship has failed to reconcile itself with the intellectual clime. Suffice it to say that through some mystery or miracle, the Jewish tradition has remained alive and vital. However, now the play of history is calling again its old drama. The facts in the matter are only too clear to a great many individuals and to some extent to all people who come into contact with the entity called Judaism. If we cannot interpret ourselves in the terms of twentieth century ideas then we may soon pass the point of no return.

There exist three prime factors or building stones from which we draw the knowledge of our own religion. These are the Bible, the Talmud, and Jewish History. I will be using all three in the coming essays and will not always refer to which one of these entities an idea of mine can be subscribed. This is due to the interrelatedness of these three factors in their actual present organization. Most probably any idea which I shall describe will be, under suitable scrutiny, found in all three of these entities; allowing me little room to elaborate on sources. A short definition of each of these factors must be here given. These definitions are to demonstrate the spirit in which the Jews approach these factors, and the method in which I shall be manipulating these factors in the essence of this work.

The Bible, the Old Testament in the vernacular, which consists of twenty-four volumes, divided into a tripartite classification: the Pentateuch or Five Books of Moses, the Prophets, and the Writings. These works comprise that half of torah known as *torah she-bichsav* (the written torah). This is to signify that their style and entire structure have been stratified and are eternally non-changeable. They were organized many centuries ago; they have not been altered in all that time; and tradition is quite adamant in stating that they were never present in any other form. This contention has never been refuted. What has given this work a unique permanence in this world of continual and perpetual change? This is the stamp of divine revelation, which is the core of the authority of this work. It is impossible to discuss this work without taking into account that it owes its entire stability to the concept of revelation. I cannot here attempt to define what one understands by revelation. We may perhaps touch upon this subject in another context. However we may personally feel concerning this subject, we can in no way dismiss its paramount connection to the Bible. The Bible, permanent in texture to its last letter, and permanent in the turbulence of history, is a product of the eternal essence which man seeks, and which he has almost always equated with Divinity.

The Talmud, *the sea of learning*, is the second half of torah, and also a contrast to the first half, and is appropriately known as *torah shel baal peh* (the oral torah). In the general form which we know it, it is written, and we are

9

often not cognizant of the fact that it is only so written due to the necessity which Jewish dispersion has implanted upon it. The core of talmudical literature is the Mishnah, completed about seventeen hundred years ago, and the large and intricate extension of this, the Babylonian Talmud, completed about two hundred years after the Mishnah. But talmudical lore by no means is constricted to these two alone. All of Midrash, all the commentaries on the Bible, all of the codes of law, and the "question and answer" texts on Jewish law; in fact all works which have any relation to the Bible and to the Jewish religious concept, from very ancient eras to those being published today, are a part of the sea of Jewish learning called the Talmud.

There are two principles of talmudic scholarship. The first is its continuity. This is known as *Masoreh*, the principle of handing down the principles from father to son, from one generation to the next. "Moses received the torah at Sinai and he passed it on to Joshua, and Joshua to the elders, the elders to the prophets, and the prophets to the judges at the Great Court." We could continue this sequence, quoted from *Avot*, with the judges handing down the principle to the tanaim (Mishnaic era), the tanaim to the amoraim (Talmudic era), the amoraim to the geonim, the geonim to the reshonim, the reshonim to the acharonim, the acharonim to the Rav Harashim and rabanim of our present day. This continuity of principle, within the varied and abundant material which was produced in each one of these intellectual eras of Jewish scholarship, is the foundation stone of the entire wisdom of the sages. Yet the Talmud is above all things neither stratified nor without an abundance of contradictions, loose-ends and varied opinions on almost any subject in the repertoire of human knowledge. This is just the manifestation of the second principle of talmud, its "oral" principle. The exact point of departure of a written hand-down and an oral one is that the first is

10

only an influence on each succeeding generation but can't be influenced by those generations, whereas the second hand-down is both influenced and influencing each succeeding generation. The father in relating the subject to the son not only hands down that which he received but also an addition of his own. This is the mastery of talmud and has made it possible to have Jewish religious principles, stable as they must be, not become encumbered with petrified and dogmatic thought and action patterns. The thought and action patterns in Judaism have indeed been pliable and this has led to the non-interrupted history of Jews. It would be fatal for one here to imply that this in any way guarantees the continuance of Judaism in the future. If this were so I would have nought whatever to write after this point. Due to the expulsion and dispersion of Jews after the end of their second commonwealth in Palestine, and due to the rising amount of arguments concerning questions of Jewish practical law, it became necessary to write down parts of the Talmud and take definite decisions in the field of *Halachah* (Jewish law). This lead to the Mishnah and the two Talmuds, Babylonian and Palestinian, and later on to the substream of codified Jewish law; a substream headed by the two principal Jewish codes; Maimonides' *Yad Hachazakah* (the "strong hand" of law) and Rabbi Jacob ben Asher's *Arba'ah turim* (the four rows or sets of law). Today one is rarely aware of the fact that talmud is oral transition, for we only encounter it in its written forms.

The Talmud is the unfurlment of the genius of man to the principles of torah; enhancing them and making them permeate into the manifold crevices of human existence.

From the viewpoint of an historian, it would be difficult to adequately state that Jewish chronological existence is manifested by different phenomena than is recorded in other historical records. From the viewpoint which the historian takes, his metaphysical bias, he sets out to determine the pattern of his history. When he has accomplished this, he then has but to insert facts, figures, names and dates into his scheme. He feels rather adamantly that it matters little what facts he inserts and that these facts can be inserted interchangeably. Yet this is not quite the case. The facts inserted do alter the picture which we are given and often change the metaphysical concept which was his basic mental criterion of understanding. History is but one of the fields which we so arrogantly feel that we have comprehension of; yet sometimes we realize that the meeting points between comprehension and incomprehension are so close together that to decide on which side of the fence we are on is most difficult.

With a framework so fickle, I attempt here yet to give a statement or two of specific attributes of Jewish history. A history of the Jews is primarily an outline of their intellectual achievements. All details which are included besides the recording of intellectual achievements are but ornaments to give proper perspective of time and place. It is necessitated to have some mundane facts to conceive the pains of birth of a Jewish intellectual activity and to conceive the process of dissemination of any new idea; to see the paths the idea must take to be accepted. Where other nations can have histories both illustrious and adventurous, the Jews have for the main been relegated to a history which is either inglorious or insignificant at its best, and deprecated and despised at its worst. It is not easy to brandish for the public approval the portrait of the scholar bent and concentrating over a volume, when it is a knight in shining armour which they so desire to see; both without and within themselves. We have one small consolation, one due only to long generations of experience; that when the knight in shining armour perishes he is "as dead as a doornail," whereas intellectual pursuits don't die and they rarely fade away.

One other rule rarely, if ever, found to be overruled in Jewish history, is the role of the minority. It is a history of a small group, usually widely dispersed and subject to the vagaries of more dominant groups. Prof. Toynbee has chosen to refer to the Jews as a "fossil" of an ancient Middle East culture. This reference has caused no small indignation among Jewish scholars of history. It may be an ill-advised term. However the term is not so untenable as the implication which one draws therefrom; this making it quite false. The implication of a fossil is that this was at one time in an opposing state, a vital and powerful state, versus the present state of lifelessness and overpowering uselessness. This can in no way be implied into Jewish existence. It has undergone no great change of course to suggest that it is today better or worse than it was two thousand years ago. If we are today a fossil then we were always a fossil. We were thus always, at least to some who so desire, an added appendage to the main stream of history. If one is wont to describe Jewish existence of old as vital and creative, then the present Jewish existence is no less so. If one is wont to describe present Jewish existence as listless and superfluous, then ancient Jewish history was no less so. Nowhere do we find that schism in Jewish history to justify a double standard of valuation. Even during the years that Jews had their own state, they were almost constantly under domination, of various types, to powerful neighbors. No, the Jews could not be accounted as having made a great success of national statehood. I don't claim that this is or was inevitable. It is a mere fact of history. For better or worse we have been compelled to remain a very minor factor in the political and social history of human existence. Yet the Jewish achievement in various marginal fields, areas which have been less coveted by the rest of humanity, has been quite illustrious. At present these fields, for the great extent within the bounds which we

13

denote *social sciences,* are somewhat undesirable and certainly little understood. It is thus not incomprehensible that our generation should find little contribution to universal society from Jewish history. Yet this need not always be so. It may yet accrue to the Jews a share of appreciation; at such time when what they value and participate in becomes more universally accepted. However, today it is still true that the Jew is a minority, both in his person and in his thought. What is worse he finds it ever more difficult to justify his marginal existence, not only to others, but to himself. We dedicate this whole work to alleviate just this difficulty of justification. I fear that not all will find contentment at the image herein depicted. We have, however, no choice but to attempt to justify ourselves. This is the albatross about the neck of every minority.

We have now, perhaps belaboredly, covered the preliminaries. We stand now as the swimmer who has assessed his surroundings and is about to plunge into the sea. The sea we will plunge into is entire existence. The length, depth and breadth of the physical sea is nought compared to that of the sea of existence. And the perils of our sea are just as engulfing. Our task is to give one a spiritual oar with which to help him paddle through this sea.

I cannot help knowing that I must fall short in this task, no matter how well I shall do. For the very task of keeping an eye on all of existence, although our main focus is on Judaism, is quite unfeasible. But one must try his best. And trying his best means that the critical analytic mind must attempt to emulate the eagle. He must attempt to have powerful wings with which to fly high above the turgid world; a broad back on which to carry fledgling ideas; an eagle's eye with which to spot the principle in any current of thought; and above all a tireless heart with which to roam wide, and to hope much and to keep the spirit within aflame.

CHAPTER I

THE SEA OF NATURE

The world in which we dwell cannot be described in a few short statements. It is felt by many that it cannot be described at all. We are present in it and are necessitated to live in it. We humans in our own integrating, so to speak, into worldly existence use processes which we call describing nature. Whether these processes, intellectual and emotional, are real comprehensions of nature, or only another form of a part of nature integrating with the general existence, is problematical. All we know is that we seek this description of nature and that it is not the least difficult of objects to achieve.

If it is difficult to describe or circumscribe all of the world at once, it is less difficult to depict. the "method of action" of the universe. By this I mean the description of the universal law of the mode of change. All that we are necessitated to prove is that there exists such a universal law, that it is possible to demonstrate and apply to all phenomena, and that this law is a true means of describing nature. To prove the first is to establish the presence of our idea; to prove the second is to confirm the validity of scope of our idea; and to prove the last is to affirm the practicality of the existence of our idea. This is, indeed, again no small task. It is, however, the one which we shall choose to fulfill.

In this mid-twentieth century era, which is our own epoch to forge a distinct history, we have reached in our scientific research into nature a unique intellectual ideology. This ideology is not a monolithic feature, but one which is of a duplex nature. Not only is it duplex, but it is also apparent that each half of the ideology is an extreme position in itself and that it is, at least superficially, a contradiction of the other half. It is this inherent contradictory attitude of the two halves of scientific knowledge which often makes this knowledge ill-comprehensible. The first half of this knowledge is the "splitting of the atom" of knowledge. The more we search into the depths of nature, the greater diversity of entities we find. The more we attempt to explicate an entity, the more prone we are to find more pertinent factors within the entity. The more we seek an encyclopaedic scope of knowledge, the more we see the infinity of the limitlessness of nature in its diversity and comprehension. The historical trend has been towards this "splitting of the atom" of each field of knowledge. There was a time when theology encompassed all extant scholarship. Then, when scholasticism brought Aristotle into western Christian society, there was a split between theology and philosophy. Thomas Aquinas for Christianity and Maimonides for Judaism attempted to heal the split, but only succeeded in postponing its acceptance. With the intellectual change of pace which ensued after the political, social and economic reorganization of society after the sixteenth century, the ax began to fall again and split knowledge. Science was divorced from philosophy. Later science itself was divided into physical science and social science. Still later a clear distinction came into existence in the physical sciences between physics, chemistry and biology, and in the social

16

sciences between sociology, economics and psychology. Today, we are all familiar with the numerous "division of labor" tendencies within all of these fields. Today also we have many added subdivisions resulting from hybrids of a gene from one traditional field and a gene from another traditional field. Bio-physics, social-psychology, and bio-chemistry are just a few perfunctory examples. It is quite clear that we now have a whole array of different intellectual fields which seem to be ever more undergoing binary fission and hybridization to create new organisms of knowledge.

This first half of scientific knowledge is almost obvious and certainly very apparent. Its complementary as well as perplexingly contradictory tendency is somewhat less obvious. Nevertheless, it is quite apparent for all those who make the minor effort to discern it. It is the tendency in scientific knowledge to see an ever more inter-relatedness or similarity of conception within the widely diversified entities. It is as if there were a common denominator for nature and the greater the other factors become split and diversified, the more is the tendency for this common denominator to approach one or unity. Not perplexing? Not a contradiction? Not extreme tendencies in opposite directions? Certainly it is! We find that a complement to splitting of ideas is a fusion of some ideas, until there seems to be a real discernible statement of extant nature which we can advocate and will be applicable to the entire universe. This fusion is of course on a different level of explanation from that of general scientific explanation; which is witnessed by many theories, laws and facts. This explanation must be sort of a theory on theories. It is necessarily much more abstract and less easily describable. It is in philosophy the idea of metaphysics and its attendant meta-language to

17

which we are alluding here. This is, however, a theory of science and whether one wishes to call it metaphysics depends on the individual. It is to attempt to harness this universalizing tendency in scientific knowledge to which we now shall converge our efforts.

* * *

In our universe we witness the strange phenomena of opposites which are coupled together and which are mutually influenced by one another. We do not always empirically see this, yet as we search more precisely into the situation, this principle unfurls ever more. The fact which is permeating every field of endeavor now, is that our world is like a set of balance scales. Just as on the scales there are always two trays hanging from the arms and it is impossible for one to change the situation in one tray without changing the situation in the other tray, so to is it in all life. Just as it is necessary for one to compensate the other tray for any change made in the first tray in order to maintain an equilibrium, so too is it in every natural phenomenon. We can only discuss concepts in pairs: action and reaction; superior and inferior; internal and external; growth and decay; good and bad; rising and falling; termination and generation; war and peace; balance and unbalance; laughter and tears; joy and sorrow; straight and curved; stationary and moving; finite and infinite; love and hate; light and dark; facile and hard. Not only does any one of a pair have no meaning without reference to the other, but one component can in no way change unless there is a compensatory change in the other.

Together with the idea of twin concepts goes the idea of equilibrium. Why such a method should exist is completely

18

impossible for one to question. All that we can state is that it exists and exists in almost all phenomena which we can analyze. Equilibrium means that one part of a situation cannot become changed without causing a change in another part of the situation to counteract the change in the entire system and cause an equilibrium of forces to remain. We do not readily know at which point an equilibrium is reached or how many equilibriums are possible in physical nature; and the problem is more complicated in social nature. Yet we do know that equilibrium is the point to which nature constantly tends to move towards and from which it is difficult for one to move nature away. In fact, many state that we never do shift from equilibrium in the total view of nature. It is just that individual parts are shifting about; and if we look narrowly only at a specific action we could tend to feel that an imbalance is arising. But somewhere in nature a complementary entity is moving simultaneously to counteract this action and maintain equilibrium.

To complete this universal idea of existence we must add that the effected action is always *equal and opposite* to the causing action. Now we can't determine which action is cause and which is effect if, as we stated, they occur simultaneously. But if we shall for explanatory purposes take one action as the cause (it may seem to us that it occurred earlier, since we were aware of it first) and state that this action lead to a certain specific movement in time and space, then the reactive complementary twin occurrence will be found to be of an equal proportion and in the opposite direction in time and space. The whole situation is analogous to the see-saw. There can be no situation where both ends of the see-saw are up or both are down. When one side goes up an equal action in proportion and opposite in direction occurs and the other end descends. There is an extreme point beyond which one end cannot rise, which means at the same position the other end cannot any longer fall. The same explanation is given to less physical phenomena within nature. There exist complementary situations. They must remain in equilibrium at all times. If one part of the equilibrium changes then an opposite and equal action occurs in the other end of the situation to compensate the entire order and keep it on an even keel.

* * *

Now this pattern can be adequately demonstrated and I shall attempt to give a few examples of its principal unfurlment in the empirical sciences, before I attempt to discuss its implications towards the human psyche.

The basis for this entire concept most probably arose from Newtonian physics, and although we must change our analytical terms from one science to another, the physical analysis remains the most concrete in our minds and the basis of analogous phenomena in other spheres.

Of Newton's three laws for the physical explanation of the universe, it is his third which states expressly our concept of equilibrium action. He states that any action in physical terms causes a reaction which is equal in intensity and opposite in direction. "The mutual actions of two bodies upon each other are always equal, and directed to contrary parts." One must here state as Newton himself showed that equal is not a term to signify equality of any individual factor (e.g. velocity, mass, acceleration), but equality of action in the whole system which leads to proportional equality among the individual factors. Thusly, we measure a certain phenomenon and by the general relatedness of other factors in the system to this one phenomenon we can mathematically deduce its measurable consequences. The important significance of this third law is that there is no real movement in physical reality. There is a shifting of factors about, a sort of changing position between dancing partners. But whatever occurs to one occurs mutually to the other in an opposite direction and in equal intensities so as to be mathematically equal to zero. We only get positive movement results by mathematical analysis of only one part of what takes place in a physical situation. We often find it necessary to do this in a given situation, but it should not blind us to the reality that we are only improvising a forward movement where none really exists.

Newton's "law of inertia," his first principle, actually amounts to the same concept. This is nought more than stating that when an equilibrium of forces is attained that this position, whether stationary or moving, is the one which is sought to be maintained by the body. It is not only the position to be maintained, but the one which cannot be altered without some outside factor's interposition. Inertia is only another way of stating that equilibrium is the end result of natural physical endeavor. When that is reached, all is in balance. All of mechanical physical analysis in daily situations amounts to the calculation of unbalanced forces upon inertia systems; calculations derived from Newton's second law and its further development to specific situations.

The biological-chemical analysis of equilibrium in nature has been developed over a long period of time. There is much empirical evidence for it and it forms the basis for our comprehension of extant organic existence. No doubt most people today are aware of the *balance of life* principle in explanation of universal organic transition. Very few could go through a high school course in biology and fail to be shown the aquarium of balanced life, a tank which contains some fish and snails, some seaweed and light, and an aerating system. Here is explained the complexities of maintaining a balance between consumption of one chemical and creation of another chemical, oxygen and carbon dioxide. Here we are imparted the knowledge that one product is both waste material and food, depending upon which end of the creation—consumption ends of the product you are on. We are given a microcosm of the organic world and shown that it is only due to the balance of factors which accrue from the diversified activities of organic material, balance in chemical and biological terms, that life can be adequately maintained on our planet. No longer is it possible for one to ask or state which is more important, animals or plants. The question is nonsense. We are in need of both and all, and if we were to lose just one factor or upset just one factor we would create an imbalance which would lead to reactionary consequences. Conservation authorities and natural biologists are constantly aware of this. It no longer becomes necessary to explain the overflowing of a river basin in supernatural terms, but as a natural reactionary consequence from ignorant methods of removing forests and natural foliage. Farm areas which yesterday were blooming today lay fallow from usurpation of the chemical ingredients, which when unreplenished, will lead to the inevitable consequences of inability to allow growth. The dissipation of certain animal life from an area has lead to the increase of other animal life in that area which would have been held in check if the balance were undisturbed. Natural biologists have lexicons full of data on the variation of rodents, insects, fish and worms and how they should be manipulated so as to prevent undesirable consequences. Undesirable here of course pertains to farmers, businessmen or mankind in general. From the standpoint of nature there is no such an entity as desirable or undesirable. What exists must remain in balance. If a factor is unbalanced then there is established a new equilibrium, inertia, and balances of forces are as real as they are in the mechanical physical world.

* * *

This principle is now an integral part of analysis in the social sciences as well as in the more theoretically developed natural sciences. In the social sciences, however, it is somewhat more difficult to demonstrate due to the preponderance of variagated occurrences and of our inadequate comprehension of these occurrences.

The analysis of economic problems is perhaps a paradigm example of equilibrium analysis in the social sphere. It would be impossible for one to discuss economic shifts and movements without a discussion of the factors which bring about an equilibrium or stabilization of the economic pattern in a given economy. The great revolution which has occurred in economic thought with the advent of the Keynesian theories of economics is a new analysis of the various factors which lead to an equilibrium in social business activities, and not a refutation of the inevitable existence of an equilibrium in those activities. The dominant economic theory until about one generation ago was the so termed "classical" theory of economics. This theory held to the view that consumption and production would inevitably be equal. They held that people would consume all that was supplied to them by entrepreneurs, since, as Say's law states, "supply creates its own demand." They, therefore, surmised that there was only one point in the economy where it could be equalized, and that was the full employment level. Since supply created will be demanded in all events and entrepreneurs are out to make as much profit as possible, they will create the greatest supply possible, that supply which takes advantage of the economic factors to the fullest extent; a point which is reached only at full employment. This was their most important analysis; and they allowed for crises in the economy as a minor adjustmental factor. The sum of the analysis is that possible production and consumption are dependent directly on one another and since one is sort of the inverse of the other they will always equal each other.

This almost mechanical analysis has been superseded by a more intricate analysis of the economics of society since the writings of Lord Keynes. The basic principle which is now espoused is that possible production and consumption are each dependent upon a different set of factors and since this is true the economic equilibrium of society can be so established as to be at numerous points, only one of which is the full employment level. In non-economic and very perfunctory terms the theory today is that consumption and its attendant non-consumption or savings are dependent directly upon the income of the community. Production, however, and its attendant increased production or investment is determined by the calculation of the possibility of a profit, or gaining from the business activity more than what it will cost. Now the calculation of these two different phenomena may prove to be equal or one greater than the other. If the two are equal then the consumption and production equilibrium in society will be at the full employment level, the point where all that could be supplied will be demanded. If the consumption phenomenon is greater than the production phenomenon than there will be an equilibrium in society which will demand greater production. This will be full-employment but will be an inflationary trend, since production is already at full employment and cannot meet the wished for consumption demands of society. If the consumption phenomenon is calculated to be smaller than the production phenomenon than there will be a deflationary trend, with the possible production being scaled down until it meets only the requirement of what is wished to be consumed. This will lead to an equilibrium of production-consumption decidedly below the full-employment level. To analyze and to find means of implementation of methods to control the economic equilibrium so as to be as close to the full-employment level as possible without either inflation or deflation is the main business of economics today.

Another very pertinent example of the balance of factors is analysis in the field of international relations. No one has been able to even commence a discussion of international politics without mentioning *balance of powers, status quo* or initial equilibrium, and unbalanced equilibrium. The analysis consists of assessment of the various power factors in a sovereign nation's existence vis-a-vis all other sovereign nations. Needless to say, this is a very intricate and unverifiable assessment due to the numerous large and small nations and due to the many fluctuating factors for power within a nation. I shall attempt to illustrate this analysis with a theory of current interest which contains certain personal reflections. It is in no way attempted to be a true or a practical study for it is a generalization about a very complicated socio-political conflict.

The poles of international relations today, at their extreme positions, are Western civilization or the Anglo-American bloc of nations, and Eastern civilization or the Russian-

Chinese Communist bloc of nations. These two poles act as magnets and tend to create a whole array of small nations dependent, to a larger or smaller extent, on the political, economic and socio-psychological ways of the magnets. Those nations which are furthest away from both poles tend to blend into a third group, when viewed in comparison to the general duplex classification, and are termed neutral nations. This term does not imply, as some might have one believe, that these nations are against war more than other nations. It simply means that the magnetic attraction—repulsion action of the twin poles is not strong enough for these nations to take definite commitments towards one of these poles; the result being that these nations decide which international sphere they will follow in each individual action instead of faithfully adhering to one sphere. Most of the statesmen who represent one of these neutralist nations believe that their hands are more free in international relations. This is, in my opinion, only an infatuated emotional evaluation, rather than the truth. For the truth remains, that they lie in the doldrums of power politics and they have the constant necessity thereof for deciding why, when and how they will take issue in any particular international problem. And should they become more powerful internally they will soon find that they will be forced to make a definite external commitment to one of the poles, or be an eventual ripe fruit for the grabbing by the stronger of the two bears who vie for universal supremacy.

The magnetic force of the two poles has somewhat diminished in the last several months and this has made international relations somewhat more explosive; what with the smaller nations now more in possession of strength to rearrange and reorganize among themselves. The twin poles have both been quite in agreement that this is not desirable, for they both cannot calculate how the rearrangements will affect their own balance sheet vis-a-vis each other. They thus find it necessary to circumscribe international action as best as possible for fear that even the smallest change will work in favor of their opponents. This has, however, not been able to completely hamper the actions of some nations which have found the status quo's continuance unbearable. The actions and reactions in the Middle East and in the satellite countries since mid-October of 1956 can only be explained in these terms.

One prominent feature stands out in this entire international political structure. That feature is the almost physical nature of the twin poles and the action which they initiate. One is the opposite of the other; we could classify one as a positive and one as a negative pole; each pole attracts entities to it of a like nature and repels those which are unlike it or like its opposing pole; each action taken by the one pole causes a reaction in the other which is certainly in the opposite direction and perhaps proportionately as great. Now it is determined exclusively by which side of the Iron Curtain one dwells in that classifying of positive and negative to the opposing twin poles will depend. To us, as really to the physicist, it doesn't matter. But what concerns us is that what is the predominant method on our side of that curtain is in reality a strict opposite to that which is the predominant method on the other side of the curtain. The general terms used to explicate this situation are multifarious and ambiguous to a high degree. I find it necessary, in order to make this a short general thesis, that I must coin and define a set of new terms. The terms I shall introduce here are *social-generating* for the Western culture and *social-degenerating* for the Eastern culture. No valuation of the worth of either system is by these terms intended. Both situations are strained or extreme ones and both are the antithesis of each other.

By social generating in our society I mean that the general method of our society in its activities is a group one rather than an individual one. The criteria and the means of accomplishing are not highly prized in or for the individual but for the group. The organization, formal or informal, real or mythological, large or small, are of paramount significance with the individual consideration running a poor second.

By social degeneration in a Communistic society I refer to the opposite phenomena. Here, of primary importance is the individual, and his criteria and methods are the predominant aspect of the social mobilization. The many social organizations of our society are broken down and referred to as capitalistic and subversive. All people become comrades and the method of finding a social goal is to enhance one's individual traits. But a society can little amount to anything in our world of interdependence between individuals, especially in an industrialized society, when each individual acts independently. So in order to keep a social stabilization the great extreme of individual initiative has been augmented by a strong state control. Somehow the individual freedom from economic and political control for each person, thus a classless society, has not been able to survive with a stable society. So the result is an almost classless and individual society where everything, down to the sewing on of a button, is controlled not by the individual, but by the state. This is the result of the great liberal credo of the eighteenth century. Freedom and equality and the rest are indeed only relative entities. And they don't exist without their opposites in our comprehension of things.

Thus an action which is for complete freedom in the extreme for the individual must result in a proportionate opposite reaction for enslavement for the individual. Freedom for the Soviet individual is the non-involvement with numerous different organizations. He must therefore, belong to just one organization which more than makes up for all the rest; that is being a citizen in his state-controlled country.

I stated that both the Western and the Eastern social patterns are extremes. Being in themselves extremes they are not really adequate equilibriums. The Soviet system causes unrest among its inhabitants who are dissatisfied with the social organization, persons who wish to crack the monolithic social organization. This type of unrest could break out into armed conflict with a large part of the people uniting to change the equilibrium of their society away from its extreme unity, individual and state. In our own society the extreme social organization consciousness of our population also causes unrest and rebellion. This rebellion is by those who wish for more individual fulfillment and less to be controlled by manifold organizations and groups. This sort of rebellion is less noticeable, since it is predominantly individuals who are continually disassociating from some social group; and these individuals do not form their own groups and become armed insurgents. But unrest is quite apparent; and one should add to quite a large extent. Maybe our society is not the best of all worlds, after all?

* * *

In this mid-twentieth century year, it would be inconceivable to discuss nature without including some remarks about psychology. There was a time when we at least fancied that we could be objective and view our surroundings as though we ourselves were not a part of them. Psychology does not allow us this luxury any more. We are now subservient to the ideas of the mind searchers who tell us that whatever we do, we do for some specific reason, conscious or otherwise, and that almost as the astrologers of old, given the proper set of facts they will delineate the actions of the organism. It's rather ironic though, how often we manage to outwit the psychologists. I feel that this must be due to the obviously overt objectiveness of the practitioners, for if they were only subjective they would be so preoccupied with themselves as never to get around to us. Perhaps it would be better that way after all. Nevertheless, our generation could use this one word of advice. Since psychology is by its very nature a bit ambivalent, just as the very life which it studies and springs from, we should not always take it too seriously. Most of all, since the more subjective we become, preoccupied with ourselves, the less objective we can be of the world about us, we can well do with a bit less application of psychoanalysis to every crook and nook of existence. Even if it may be true, must every Dr. Jekyll who crawls into his corner be aware of a Mr. Hyde's presence?

It was the theories of Dr. Sigmund Freud which brought into the world of comprehension the mechanism which applies our concept of equilibrium, balance of entities, and compensation for each action to the realm of the psychic. His analysis consists of the principle that the psychic existence consists of the equilibrium of all the sets or pairs of factors (we have not been able to completely establish that these always work in pairs, but we have established certainly that certain groups of mental actions compensate for each other) and that if this equilibrium is disturbed it causes repercussions in that psychic existence. To be able to adequately comprehend this mechanism we must take into account that many of these compensations and reorganizations take place in an unobservable realm, the unconscious. Only when we take into account these unknown, to the individual, actions can we interpret many of the actions of the human being. Freud discovered the unknown unconscious, but he has not been the only one to chart this area. Many have contributed to our comprehension thereof, and there still is quite a bit of it which remains shrouded in the dark realms of mystery. To illustrate how this has developed in practice I will allow a psychologist to take over my pen. I could not invent any more succinct examples than these.

Quote from *What Is Science*, Newman, James R., ed. New York 1955 (Simon and Schuster), *Psychoanalysis* by Fromm, Erich. P. 364-365.

"Two simple examples may help to clarify the point. A man who is constantly bragging, boasting, belittling others is perhaps aware of himself as a masterful, superior person. What he is not aware of is that in reality all these feelings of power and superiority are only compensations for the very opposite. Deep down he feels weak, helpless, childish, and at the very moment when he tells us "look here what a great guy I am," he is really praying "do not let them find out that I feel like a helpless child." If we were to investigate further, we might find that this man feels like a helpless child because he has never overcome a deep fixation to his mother, a passive attachment which, normal for the child, is weakening for the

31

man and should long since have been severed. His aim is probably still to be nursed, cared for, protected, admired by mother, and just because of his attachment, he feels like a child and hence weak and inferior. He may, in a more extreme case, have acquired the habit of compulsive drinking; only when under the influence of liquor can he overcome the feeling of powerlessness and at the same time the drinking is a substitute for his wish to be nursed and indulged by mother. The deeper one searches into the unconscious, the more links one uncovers in the chain of behavior.

In the other example of unconscious motivation a young student, brilliant, intelligent, conscientious, gets so frightened before an examination that he is almost paralyzed and jeopardizes his whole career. He is particularly frightened when the examiner is a teacher whom he does not like. Otherwise, the young man shows no signs of fear, has no feeling of inferiority, and is always poised and sure of himself in his relationship to older people or contemporaries. If one seeks the reasons of his examination fear, one finds at first an intense rage against the examiners, and especially the ones whom he does not like. Behind that rage is a feeling that it is an unbearable humiliation that he should be forced to submit to authorities who can decide about his career. Without going into the history of this intense rebelliousness against authority, it may be said that his anxiety, of which he was conscious, replaced and covered up what he was not aware of—a deadly rage which he had to repress because to show and express it would have made his position untenable. Here, as in the first example, a person is aware of his feeling, but not aware of what causes it."

We could, if our inclination so desired, continue this discussion ad infinitum. I have not brought up the several fields which I discussed till here to illustrate my personal scope but to illustrate the idea of the universe which has become the paramount point of comprehension of the reality of its existence. It is much to be desired that the reader should insert some illustrations which will be in his own realm of experience. It will make more salient the conclusion which we shall here organize.

The world in which we live has become to our understanding an awesome *equation*. There is not really one world but two halves to the world. When you distort an entity in one half you will automatically distort an equal complementary entity in the other half. We have expressed this phenomenon in an iron law. This is the law of the *conservation of energy*. In this short phrase is enclosed the full significance of all our endeavors. We cannot deduce the possibility of any real change in our world from nature itself. The unconscious sphere of physical action is chemical reaction. And when we behold the total panorama we find the resultant change to be equal to zero. It consists entirely of the rearrangement of the factors, factors which themselves become infinite in their number, variations, and methods, nevertheless demonstrate the consequence that they result in change of no significance. No matter what your boundaries are in the material which you are dealing with do we not find this result? It may be the area of the microcosmic entities of the atomic structure of materials or the cellular structure of organic materials. It may be the somewhat superficial boundaries in our everyday existence of classes, organizations, institutions, categories, societies, and historical eras. And it may be the limitless boundaries of the entire universe; the fascinating and enticing realm of the boundless heavens and the numberless stars. In all do we hapless beings search for something which we can hardly perceive and even less explain. And in all areas the result is conclusively the same. There exist positive and negative factors which equalize and nullify each other. The sum total of all construction is equal to the sum total of all destruction. The sum total of all saving is waste. The total of all progression is regression. The sum of the total is nothing.

Or is it nothing? Surely if this law were to reign supreme there would be no need for me to write anything else at this point. Indeed there would be no reason apparent to have written thus far. Is not the world a stabilized entity which must always be stable? Is not every action a justified one since it invariably causes a reaction just as great in all dimensions and therefore is as nought were done at all? I don't think that that realm known as the human race can be quite satisfied with such an austere conclusion. Not to even determine the chaos and havoc which a strict institution of such a doctrine to man's own social order would entail, we cannot even allow ourselves to feel that there exists no reality except this one. Maybe we are egoistic concerning ourselves, but we cannot find it possible to state that whatever we do is for nought. We cannot succumb to an equation where nothing changes but the hour hand of the clock. The question which naturally arises is whether it is at all possible to state that man has a possibity to countervail or circumvent in some manner or area this all inclusive law of nature. If we should fail to find a loophole then the nihilism of all periods in history will be justified by default of a case against it.

CHAPTER II

THE CREATIVE INSTINCT

There exists an area of pursuit and occurrence which is quite dear to us. It is so because it is our very own human endeavors. Human endeavor unfolds into many varied and colorful enterprises. It is for us to attempt to find, if possible, the universal ideas which can be associated with these endeavors. It is also within our task to establish what relationship these human efforts have with the realm of nature which we have already at length discussed.

Human life can only be viewed to us through one medium, and that is history. Through it and the unique awareness of it that the human organism has can we behold and describe what poets have called "der menschliche Schmerz." We are not going now into particular facts or trends in history. We are approaching it from the viewpoint of a comprehension of what it is and what is man's relationship to it.

* * *

Within our environment and our experiences we are aware of a movement, a change, a substitution of events from one time to another. We are aware that tomorrow holds in store for us some new experiences, and that yesterday was quite different from today. This change takes place even if we are not active in causing it. For reasons which I shall attempt to discuss fully, man has sought to become an intimate part of this movement and change. He has, in his actions, attempted to become the responsible agent for the past and the maker of the future. Therefore, he has developed methods through which he can gain understanding and, he hopes methods to shape past and future events. Yet somehow he feels that he is conducting a losing engagement. He views the past and says to himself, "did I wish for the past to have been so conducted? What can I do about it now that the past has been as it is?" And when he views the future he is just as perplexed. He contrives to set up a path that future history should tread, but he continually ponders whether the unfurling history will travel down the path that he has established as his preference. Thus, history is a unique human intellectual endeavor, wherein he feels both a certain inevitability and a certain compulsion to be its master. He feels his life is like a swiftly flowing river, continuous and regular, which yet he must master by building a boat with which he can navigate his own way through the tides and currents of his all surrounding river. It is history which reveals to us that man has hopes for something more than a futile existence as a balanced mechanism of continuously equalized actions.

I wish here to state a fact which may not be obvious to all observers. This is that history and the contemplation of history is a peculiar activity limited to human beings. History as such, recognition of past events and future probabilities, is only such to the minds of human beings. No animal or other entity has an "historical conscience."

It is empirically true that it doesn't much matter to an animal what occurred in the past or will occur in the future. We can theoretically satisfy almost any animal well, if we understand his biological and psychological makeup, with a unit routine of activities. The animal will hardly feel compelled to seek some new activity, since he did this yesterday. A witness to this fact is that we can keep animals contented in the monotonous existential conditions of a zoo. These aniamals all exist in time and must have had histories, individual and group. Yet it concerns none of them to inquire of how their ancestors conducted themselves or of how the future will or should be generated. It is an exclusive domain of man to question, worry, doubt, and manipulate in the vast stretches of time which we call past and future. He it is who seeks to establish the authenticity of facts and events. It is he who cannot allow himself to forget his own history and continues all manner of devices for recording it; devices oral and written, ritualistic and symbolic, to help him maintain an awareness of the path which he has already trodden upon. It is he who seeks to correlate, organize and find trends in the isolated occurrences and reoccurrences in the wake of recorded and unrecorded events. He it is, who cannot find tranquility unless he can satisfy for himself the why of history, of existence, of all events that have and will take place. That this "historical conscience" is peculiar to man and also universal in all human beings is not disputable. Why man has such an urge to be concerned with history is quite disputable. The explanation can vary along the entire range of speculative areas between the poles of natural psychology to supernatural idealism. I haven't found it necessary for me to accept any one explanation to this question. It may prove inconsequential which explanation is more valid. For these explanations serve primarily as a rationale of a phenomenon which is elemental to human existence and needs no rationale. All I require is that we note this unique human experience.

From where, may I be so bold as to inquire, does man receive this attitude and concern for historical events? And, to further inquire, what does he intend to do with his over-abundant curiosity for his surroundings; past, present and future? What is it that causes this urge to know to be so powerful and universal in man?

Man has within him an instinct, a natural demeanor, or if you wish a special ability which is unique to him alone in all creation. This entity I shall call, for sheer simplicity's sake, *the creative instinct*. It is to man that it has accrued the ability to take from his environment and implant his own signature thereupon. And this is not just an activity which he may engage in if he so desires. Quite the contrary is the case. He is forced by the nature of his very existence to be a creator, a builder, a generator, an initiator to the world in which he has been placed. He alone of all phenomena finds no pleasure in life which has already been lived. He alone of all creatures will not be satiated with one monolithic routine of life. He finds himself compelled to create continually something new, something different, something unique. It is only when he has touched the unique, experienced the unknown, encountered the unmasterable that he can find his peace with the world. He searches through every crook and nook of existence that he can possibly wedge himself into, physically and spiritually, to engulf it and to implant his own ideas therein. He at no time will be satisfied with that which he created yesterday. Yesterday it was something unique; however, now it is just another part of the environment which he encounters and is therefore as old as the universe itself. Only when he touches on something new, something which he can claim is the result of his own efforts and methods does he feel exhilirated in the sense of accomplishment. This is a *Drang nach Neues*. Even the most simple of people are not satisfied with yesterday's newspaper. So too, people as a rule are not satisfied with yesterday's world. Always there is something, somewhere that must be done; a place where one can create out of the pure depths of his own imagination something which has not been present to his eyes before.

Coupled with the creative instinct, and complementary to it, is the *control instinct*. Here also is a unique undertaking of the human being. He is not contented with a world which is regulated by methods which he is unaware of. He wishes to know these methods intimately and to be able to manipulate them in a fashion which he desires. He seeks to be the master of all natural phenomena so that all that occurs will be regulated at his own caprices, and not in mysteries which he must be wary of. He feels terribly disturbed at any instance in which he finds that he cannot determine what that instance shall encounter.

And even when he is creating and when he is in control of certain natural occurrences, he is unsatiated. Yet he wants something more. He wants eternity; universal and interminable eternity. He wants that his life and his actions upon this universe shall be written in indelible ink. He wants that which he has created to be permanent, incapable of being obliterated. He feels that only then has he reached a purposeful existence when he has gained control of his environment to such an extent as to be able to create something unique which will be of eternal significance. And we all strive towards this goal in our lives.

It is for this reason that man is so preoccupied with

history. It is his underlying ideal that he cannot find the methods to achieve creation, control and permanence unless he investigates how life has been conducted. It is only within the lessons which have already been learned by the human race, so he feels, that he can discover the items that man has created, the methods that man has developed to control nature, and the areas where the eternal has been reached. And he feels that if he achieves his goals he not only will be able to forge his destiny but will be able to justify his past. He will truly feel that his is not a life lived in vain.

* * *

Thus he views the world in a fashion which is quite different from that which natural laws tell us concerning that world. The fundamental word—concept of the human race to history is the word *progress*. Nowhere are we willing to accept life unless we can perceive some significant change for the better. The watchword of almost any historian, no matter how diversified one's topics and concepts may be, is the progress of events over a period of time. The life of today is not to be just a mere repetition of that of our forefathers, but to be something better or greater. And our progeny is to be left with an existence which will be, to the best of our ability, better than our own.

Now this idea is not a new one which has been generated in the nineteenth century, as many may believe. This concept of the forward movement of society or human civilization is just as old as man himself. No human society which I have ever heard of has had for a social goal a complete stagnation of all its social processes. I doubt whether such a society ever existed, or if such a society were exhumed, it would deserve the title of being human. The concept of an ever greater fulfillment of the human raison d'etre is a natural outgrowth of its fundamental instinct to create. If we actually do create something new we are certainly progressing.

It is not the concept which was instituted in the nine-teenth century, but a change in the application of the concept and in the interpretation of the concept.

The nineteenth century witnessed the flowering of the Darwinian concept of evolution as the process of natural change in the bio-physical world. This concept was later applied also to the geo-physical world and is also now a basic theory in the field of cosmology. The theory is best explained by comprehension of the actual system to which it is analogous. That actual system is the growth of an organism from the microscopical unit cell into a large complicated and diversified organism through a period of time. The difference between the parent cell and its multi-numerous offspring is often very great in design and function, and certainly the resultant organism is of infinitely greater dimensions and diversity than its somewhat un-distinguishing originator. What is significant in this context is that a cell as such, when examined, could hardly be able to indicate to us just what sort of an organism it has intentions of becoming. All animal cells are, in principal parts, almost peculiarly alike. Only under duress of accumulation of a large amount of empirical evidence do we know that only certain cells will lead to procreation; only when these cells have been adequately processed, and they only will result in an organism which is strikingly similar to its parent organism.

This, say the evolutionists, is the design of the world. It commences with a very small entity, atom, molecule, cell

41

or what you so desire as the unit originator, and commences a period of growth until it flowers into a universe. It is quite a poetic theory and gives one a sentimental feeling concerning his world similar to that which one has for his own child. Maybe the world is a bit older than he is, but it is still nothing more or less than just a slightly mixed up adolescent who has yet to mature and stop being so conflicting and contradictory a place to dwell in.

The ancients certainly never had such an infatuate theory concerning the universe. In fact they would never consent to such a theory which used "progress" in the natural order. The world was a very constant place to dwell in according to the ancients. They did not completely ignore the possibility to institute some change for some greater comfort in the world. But these were not said to constitute a progress of the natural order. Progress and controlled betterment for the ancients consisted entirely of the betterment of the non-physical elements of his universe. It was in spiritual and intellectual attainments that man found some noticeable creation. It was only in what has been called, in generalization, man's higher values which were emphasized as those which would evolutionize or change steadily for the better. Only in this field could he ever agree with his descendants that it is worthy for man to strive, for he could therein achieve.

Now it would be somewhat disastrous for my intellectual reputation, whatever that may now be, if I would here openly renounce the theory of evolution. It has by all means become a highly accepted theory in today's world. But I shall not shirk from here questioning that theory and even, in more than one way, attacking its validity. For the logical sense of our scientific evidence tells us that the theory of evolution, indeed our entire human concept of progress is nought but an optical illusion.

This illusion stems from the perception of certain facts and the explanation of them with man's ideal of progress; and its acceptance is the result of an obvious generalization from these more ascertainable facts to the universe. The facts most of import are the biological growth pattern of an organism and the so-termed growth of the world's civilization, especially in the last one hundred years. The biological typology has been shown. The growth of civilization is a view espoused by historians. It is the Hegelian view of history. It is the pictorialization of the world's culture progressing along a road which is ever winding upward. If this road is somewhat jagged and irregular this is not to signify a lack of progress. This is only due to the inherent process, as Hegel laid it out himself. It is a result of the thesis-antithesis conflict which arises at each point in history and results in a synthesis which is not only a sort of compromise of the two, but entails the best features of the two and is therefore a stronger entity than the previous entities. The synthesis then takes on the title as a new thesis which somehow mysteriously must create or find existing an antithesis and the process continues. The result is progress. And the most significant fact to prove this has been human life in the last one hundred years. It is indeed possible to state categorically, that the fortunate old gentleman who is today celebrating his centennial of human life has witnessed in his century more change in society than would have been possible had he lived for a period five thousand years previously. Our clocks still tick at the same rate as before but our history seems to be increasing its pace by almost geometrical proportion. Why this is so I won't venture to attempt to answer. It is a most challenging occurrence and if history should condescend to allow our slowly working imaginations to keep up with it, I should hope that we could give some adequate explanation. Suffice it to state that the record is not a meagre one for the last century and it has led to the added enhancement of the evolutionary theory. How could we disagree with progress when we see progress occur so often in our own lives?

The generalization of this concept was accomplished, commencing with Darwin's application of the Hegelian system to the way animals exist, from one system to another until we don't think twice about explaining a subject in its "history" or evolutionary trend. Indeed, today we have two methods which seem to prevail in every explanational situation. The one is "evolution" and the other is "psychology." And paradoxically enough these two major-domos of our civilization are in direct contradiction to each other in their principal suppositions.

* * *

The theory must remain an illusion since the law of nature is none other, as far as we have been able to discern, than the iron law of the conservation of energy. The entire universal phenomenon is but a continuous flux of particles with an equal balance between positive and negative charges. And such a system does in no way allow for a progressive alteration of its factors. Now the illusion as such may be due to several differing causes in our weak comprehension of the changes in the universe. It may be due to the element "time" acting as the culprit. For the equalization of the various factors may not occur in the same time period. We, in our folk-ways, state this by saying that each period breeds the seeds for the next period. The seeds are in actuality the bridge which connects the two halves of the balance system. It would thus be perhaps true that our universe is now in a so called generative age and perhaps for some time to come. It may be true that this period has been continuing since recorded historical time and led us to the conclusion that it always would be thusly. But the logic of nature intervenes and says that the seeds of the degenerative period are being now fostered so that the balance of forces in the world will be restored. The conservation of energy states that we cannot receive without giving. Again the illusion may be due to a less disastrous cause. It may be that we have failed to adequately investigate both sides of the coin of nature. If this is so then we are not even now living better than our forebears, but just seeing those facts which give us reason to feel better off and ignoring those which at the same time are causing us greater hardship. Or a final cause may be a caprice of nature itself which allows us to see with greater facility the constructive aspects of her organization rather than the destructive aspects. In this case we are but shifting the blame from our own psychic to some inherent secret of nature. If this could be so then we are indeed involved in a most vicious scheme, which no matter how we should strive, we would never be able to apprehend.

Thus the proof which the prosecuting attorney has brought for evolution, the biological typology and the historical evaluation, can be accounted for by the defending attorney. The biological theory must be illusive for we pointed out the peculiar fact that the cell only matures into a particular organism, which, in generalized terms, we know to be as the parent organism. The mind questions why does the cell find it necessary to mature and will mature into only one prototype? Why should not each germ-cell develop into an organism of completely unique species according to its own inclinations? What connection exists between the original cell and the ultimate conglomeration of cells which causes the one to mature along a definite path to the other? The answer lies in the concept of potentiality. The minute single germ-cell has a potential to develop into a given organism and therefore cannot deviate from becoming that organism. Thus the cell in its process of maturation to organism is not progressing at all. It is only revealing its potential into an actual. What has possibility to be achieved, is achieved. Nothing more nor less. Even if we should find it conducive to generalize from this organic process to the entire universe and find it adequate to explain that universe as the maturation of a single atom or molecule, it would be inherently true that no progress in that universe has been achieved. It has only been that the potential universe which was within the original kernel was unfurled into an infinite number of kernels which we know as the universe now. What we are saying is that the sum total of the energy released by the kernel must be the sum total of the energy therein and not more. The difference entails only a change in the amount of space occupied or even present. This is, if valid, a great difference but not a progressional difference but a changed manifestation. For it means only an extension outward of what was previously held in more confined quarters. Since the total universal energy now is infinite then the total in the kernel was also infinite. Thus the process itself does not add or change the situation in the least. And our progress is nothing but the identification of a natural maturation process, if that. To equate evolution as progress would thus be illusionary. What is most probably more important is that evolution, if scientifically satisfactory, will give us no greater comprehension of the origin of the universe, as it usually purports to do. For the process which an entity undergoes in which no measurable change takes place cannot give us even a clue as to the origin of that entity. Our only valid conclusion might be that it has an infinite existence and no terminal points in time. Could it be possible that we have undergone five thousand years of history only to conclude the reverse of what we have always believed; that we are mortal and have definite termination points and that the world is immortal and has no termination points?

As to the Hegelian view of history as proof of progress and evolution to higher areas, we can only offer as opposite evidence, its philosophical opposite. Its opponent is Existentialism, and it could be none other. Both of these philosophies are very abstract organizations which cause the most learned of scholars perplexities. The Existentialist is in reality the twentieth century reaction to the Hegelian of the nineteenth century. And the Existentialist uses as a paradigm process psychology in protest to the theory of evolution of the nineteenth century Hegelians. Each is an extreme pole of scholarship, and, in relation to each other, one is a positive pole and the other a negative one. I don't intend to insinuate that I understand these fields to any extent. I certainly haven't as yet attempted to extricate any of the many knots which these philosophical fields have caused to men of vastly greater intellectual abilities than I have privilege to possess. I merely insert them in this essay to draw some of the generalizations which arise from them and to demonstrate from these that even in the world of ideas there exists a balance of powers. What the Hegelian draws from his process of evolution was progress towards something better or constructive growth. What the Existentialist concludes from his psychological process is progress towards something worse, or destructive growth.

This conclusion seems to me to be a result of his viewing the conscious-unconscious process in the strict Freudian sense. The Freudian showed to the world that it was no more possible for us to categorically state that this person is normal and that another is abnormal. He demonstrated that each individual has a conflict within himself or something which we generally call abnormal. It is this destruction of the demarcation line of the terminational boundaries of normal and abnormal which has caused us so much consternation within the field of psychology. The fundamental process involved is universal, and yet is quite unpopular to our values. We abhor conflict and are not willing to concede that it may be, especially within ourselves, a necessity. The Freudian conclusions of this process, which were investigated, was that this conflict was a sort of hindrance or liability in the human being or a destructive characteristic. The Existentialists have generalized from this concept and feel that all of life is essentially the process of degeneration in progress and they symbolize this existence as a "dismal abyss." For those who may be interested in keeping Freud without having resort to accept Existentialism, I venture here to add that we can accomplish this by redefining our words normal and abnormal. We only feel that a conflict or disturbance is abnormal because we have been wont to call it so. But now we are aware that conflict, and contradiction are naturally part of existence, and whether external or internal to man, we could define them as normal. What is abnormal then is only where the balance between the conflicting twin factors is upset to cause unbearable conflict, unbearable in relation to the constitution of the individual, a biological factor, or to the constitution of his life, a sociological factor. We can achieve an understanding of affairs without either Hegelianism or

Existentialism; in fact it may be necessary to disregard both. Nevertheless, if Hegelianism is offered as a proof of progress in the usual optimistic sense, then Existentialism is offered as a disproof of progress in that sense.

We must remain with the conclusion which we so belaboredly developed in the outset of this work. That conclusion, the conservation of energy, makes progress in regard to natural phenomena an illusion.

* * *

Yet man does have a very definite desire to create, to control and to progress within his environment. And we must ask the question whether he has ever created something new which did not result in a repercussion of reactionary forces which nullified his creative act. We must attempt to find an area where man could be able to control natural forces. And we must attempt to demonstrate that his ideal of progress is not a complete hallucination.

The fulfillment of this inquiry is not very simple. We have shown that certainly man requires these processes to be accomplished. He not only requires it in himself, but he also requires it almost invariably of nature. For this reason only can he institute such an idea as evolution. And although we have quite a bit of factual material to deal with when we deal with nature, we must admit that in relation to nature evolution could be only a process of extension and not one of creation. We fondly hope that in relation to ourselves, our lot is not so gloomy and that we do create. I can only arouse a possible response to these questions and not answer in either direction myself. In this connection we must delimit more precisely what it is that we seek and in what realms we delve in, and then ask ourselves what human activities might be able to be classified as fulfillments of our ideals.

What we seek to create is universal law against particular law. Particular law states that all that is necessary to be comprehended or perhaps all that is possible to be comprehended is the functioning of a particular set of factors and the fashion in which they compensate with each other. Each set in the infinite number and type of factors act as they so desire otherwise. That there are infinite type of entities is not to be denied. But that there is no connection between differing actions can perhaps be denied. Have we not created theories which are intended to explain their universal aspects? Does not the electro-magnetic theory of energy explain many diversified physical actions and portray some inherent universal character? And our interest is to extend this theory in addition to the quantum mechanics and the theory of relativity onto a higher plane which will reveal in one theory the complete universal aspects of all physical phenomena. We seek the universal aspects of our universe and can we state that we have at all failed to attain them?

We seek to have a control of the equalization function in nature. It is our desire to determine at what time and in what proportions these changes occur. And can we state that we have at all failed to achieve even a drop of mastery over nature? Are not our sciences and our arts some type of creation of our own to give means to control nature and implement a determination of what and how and when that nature shall function? We admit that control cannot be now in any way complete, but can we deny that we have any means for control?

Above all we seek eternal implementation against ephemeral changes. And here also there is evidence that we could seek as proof. The ideas that man has evolved in recorded history, are these entities either ephemeral or repercussions of some natural factor other than man's will? Are these ideas in any way necessitated to become extinct and degenerate as is the necessity of all natural generation? It is true, as stated once before, that ideas also come in polar pairs and that due to the immense pressure at either pole we attempt to keep away from the extremes and congregate more in the central neutral or compromise areas. This is due to the fact that our ideas are invariably ones dealing with nature and therefore within their tenets must reveal the natural process. Nevertheless, one finds it difficult to state that ideas die or even fade away. To demonstrate what is the opposite of ideas and compensating—balancing entity with them is even more problematical. Thusly, even if the physical-natural universe defies all that we hope for it, we ourselves are perhaps demonstrations of those things which we value. It therefore becomes rather obvious that if we hope to create in this world it could be possible only in the intellectual and ethical-spiritual areas which seem to be in themselves originally a working of the human mind.

* * *

Now I think it is possible for us to survey the underlying consequence of all of the interplay of activities in life. It may be that the fashion that I have chosen to describe this world has been inadequate. This may be due to an inability to convey clearly my ideas. It most probably will be in part due to a most difficult task of extricating general rules, which if rules, must be of a dogmatic nature, and an unwillingness on my part to be very dogmatic. I would here add that that dogmatism would have been present had I strictly defined my principal terms: equality, balance, creation, and control. Since I did not strictly define these, nor always use them in a similar active sense, although I did use them always in a similar vein, there is the result that the principal ideas were at times submerged in fogginess.

Be that as it may, I think that it was clearly stated that two realms of existence are manifest. It has truely been attempted on my part to extricate these two and place them into differing categories. It would be fallacious, however, for me to insinuate that these realms are in reality separated and unconnected. They are in fact interwoven and inter-locked in every action and every motion of the human being. They are so conjoined and united on every plain of our organic presence that it is, for all practical purposes, impossible to determine the limits or specifics of either entity in the structure or function of the human organism. Thus the description of either entity must remain somewhat allusive. Nevertheless, these realms are very well represented and they are very zealous forces within the human being. What is of greatest consternation to us is that these realms by their inherent implications are striving for opposite objectives. The creative instinct or spirit of the human race is after a man-made change or implementation within the universe. He wishes most specifically for an imbalance of existence which will lead to the institution of that which he deems more advised. He wishes for the power of manipulation of worldly phenomena so as to control its structure and function; to alter, if possible, that structure and function; and to realign them within the conjecture of his imagination. At the same moment, the realm of nature is universally opposed to any of these considerations. It wishes for nought but to remain in its equilibrium and exhorts violently against those who seek to alter its tranquility. It is a practical business man. It states categorically that it refuses to sell without recourse to payment. The payment must be commensurate with the value of the purchase. And here I present to you the source of our universal human conflict; conflict both internal and external. Man has stated his goal of worldly domination and creation and nature has stated her iron law of permanent balance. Neither is willing or has the ability to surrender its position. Yet both cannot, even through the wildest ramifications of the imagination, be satisfied at the same time in the same place. And if one strives within those areas where nature has established a tenacious hold he is bound for a series of clashes, counteractions and disappointments. The question remains in what areas has nature not established a tenacious and dogmatic grip on existence. It is at this juncture that religion commences. It is in dealing with this conflict of interests, in its resolution and its apprehension that we must evolve a religious weltanschauung. And I think that it is in the propensity that religious institutions deal with this universal conflict in man that we can justify religion as such in the twentieth century, and perhaps even justify individual religions and their dogmas. Whatever opinion may be established concerning these issues, I have chosen to make these considerations, the world of nature and the creative instinct, as the foundation for comprehension of the spirit of Judaism. It is, in my humble estimation, the resolution of these conflicting tendencies which is of paramount significance in the Jewish religion and which is dealt with in a most unique fashion therein.

CHAPTER III

IN THE BEGINNING

The reflections which have preceded this chapter were not entirely constructed from viewing life as it is now lived. I will attempt to show that these concepts are integral at the very outset of comprehension of parts of the Chumash (the Pentateuch). Indeed, it was in reflections upon passages and details of the Chumash that I first developed, perhaps rather crudely, these concepts, and it remains towards that Biblical scholarship that I intend to apply these theories. I hope, thereby, to extinguish some of that almost fairytale like attitude of people today towards the Chumash, and particularly towards the first chapters thereof concerning Creation, and to portray some of the significance which these chapters depict for man. It is not the Chumash which has not the ability to give, but we who haven't the ability to grasp. To establish a synapse between the two, one must interpret the language of the other. This will perhaps be my main task here. I will also attempt to discuss the purpose of life for which man so staunchly seeks an explanation; the goal of it all. "Contemplate therein and recontemplate therein, for all lies therein."

* * *

The first sentence of the Bible reads, in my translation thusly: "At the outset, the Divine created the Universal and the Universe." Creation consisted of an initiatory introduction of the *materia prima* into existence, and thereafter an extension of this into diversified forms. The materia prima consisted of a duplex existence, the Universal entity which is a non-material existence, and the Universe which is the natural material existence. Now these constituencies contained the potential for all of future existence within them and after their introduction there was no more creation from non-existence. There was only a period of formation of the created potential into an actual; the formation from the "clay" into the "utensil." This generative process took place only in the Universe, not in the Universal, and all of "the tale of Creation" (Maaseh Bereashit) deals only with this aspect. Only one small exception exists and this is the introduction of the Sabbath; an exception which we shall deal with in a separate chapter.

With the second Biblical sentence we commence the unfurlment of the Universe. The sentence states what are the primary attributes to the Universe. "And the Universe consisted of *time* and *space*, and of the "abysmal darkness," a simile for the degenerative force, and of the "divine spirit hovering on water," a simile for the generative force. These are the four primary elements of the universe. Time and space are infinite in their extent and immutable in their functioning. They certainly do not follow the general rule of nature of growth and decay. They either are infinitely and continuously in change or movement or they are at all times stationary and unchanging. It is according to the definition one renders to time and space which will determine which position is the more applicable. According to the relativity theory it would seem that time and space are only results of interaction or concurrent action of physical force-mass entities and thusly time and space are in reality stationary and unchanging, with physical movements constituting change. Thus without physical movement there would be no movement of time.

The rest of nature, as we know it, responds to the degenerative and generative processes. As we attempted to show in preceding discussions, these tend to equalize each other. The Biblical phrases which I feel are stating this fact are difficult ones and are variously interpreted. The phrase "darkness upon abyss" signifies to me the destructive and void-vacuum aspect of nature, and the phrase "a divine spirit upon water" signifies the constructive and growth aspect of the Universe.

It is a primary ordinance of faith that the world came into being *creatio ex nihilo*, "substance from void." Therefore, all phenomena which we know to exist at present were created and were not eternally present. Thusly time, space, generation and degeneration were created by the Divine and I have placed them into the words of the Bible; a spot I have not found others to install them into. Now the word void or nothing in this phrase causes some perplexity and a too dogmatic and literal interpretation thereof will cause confusion and misunderstanding of many of the commentaries on creation. The perplexity arises, I believe, from an immature grasp of the whole concept of infinity. Infinity is reached when we reach one of two points, zero or one. At the zero point we have infinity of voidness and at the one or unity point you obtain infinity of existence. Now both of these points are not obtained in nature. Nature is not truly nothing and not truly a unit infinity of existence. It exists, but exists in complexity and in multidimensions. However, Divinity, exists in infinite unity and to our own comprehension infinite voidness. Divinity is infinite existence which transcends all of natural conflict and disharmony and is unity in purpose and function. Also Divinity is non-nature and non-existential in natural terms (this being a corollary of the first statement) and thus, we who are natural objects and can perceive only natural existence must state that in relation to nature Divinity is an infinite void. Creation was creation from nothing in relation to ourselves as focal point, but creation from infinite unity with Divinity as focal point. Thusly, within our creatio ex nihilo dictum, we can comprehend Rabbi Eliezer the Great's, statement that the heavens were created from "the light of His garment, and the earth from "the snow beneath His throne of glory" as metaphors of the extension of existence from the Divine being; a statement which Maimonides failed to comprehend. (See Guide to the Perplexed, Pt. II Chapt. XXVI.)

Also stated previously was the fact that time was created, or at least exists as part of created phenomena. In the development of the Universe from its initial potential existence into its ultimate diversified conglomeration of existences, a period of time had to be transcended. The Biblical statement thereof, is that a seven day time period elapsed between the initial and the ultimate universal structure. The Talmud states also that there was a ten-fold phase to this construction; "With ten statements the world was created." These ten phases correspond to a change in the spacial development of the universe. In each phase there was an alteration in the space occupancy of the previous phase, until the ultimate complex and multidimensional space-matter Universe was established. The Biblical account of the extension of time and space in the formation of the world testifies that it was incumbent to creation that time elapse in the fabrication towards a mature entity. The original appearance was from no-time, but the propagation thereof was within time. It need not be much developed upon that the amount of time elapsed in the traditional account and that of so-called "modern scholarship" is in small disparity. It is not easy to obtain a compromise figure between seven days and several billion years, the present hypothetical figure for the fulfillment of universal development. The whole reason for this disparity is perhaps due to our inability to comprehend the element time in the first place. Our figure for the very long age of universal development stems from observation and theorizing concerning universal material functioning. We have determined that certain changes take certain specific lengths of time and for those changes to become so significant as to form a myriad existence would take such a long sequence of time elapsation. But we have no evidence that the functional changes could not occur equally for a shorter real duration of time, or even for a longer one. There is no law which can be stated that determines what length of time an action should dissipate. Our only criterion of determination is an empirical one and is based on our observation over phenomena of different types on different occasions. Does this mean that time is only an illusion? I don't really think so. But it certainly portents that time is relative; relative to the occurrences with which it is associated and used by the human mind as a yardstick for measurement and determination. With time a relative relationship occurrence, we could feel less uncomfortable concerning the disparity in the lengths of time in the "story of creation." If relativity implies nothing more (as it most certainly does) than the fact that our criteria are not so absolute and ultimately individually determinable, it would suffice to render us less enthused for the significance of facts and figures. What becomes significant is the plan or system which is beheld.

Concerning creation we have determined the design and system of its development in time and space. In relation to individual facts within the plan one has to take what the modern religious philosophers like to call "the leap of faith." This is true for whatever set of facts you wish to adhere to, whether traditional or various scientific data. For the total picture in its detail seems beyond the possibility of true comprehension even to science and if one is determined to have a complete rationalization of the process he must insert certain facts and processes which he believes in only because he has belief in them and without further positive grasp. With this rather equivocal statement on a subject which causes so much heated debate, namely the length of the duration of creation, I close this initial report. Of primary import here were the facts of *creatio ex nihilo*, the initial creation of the potential Universe, and the consequent construction into an actual with the elapsement of a period of time. These are fundamentals of Judaism and denial of them is incompatable with faith in it.

* * *

When the task of universal construction was nearing completion, there was instituted a peculiar entity. This entity was constituted of two differing forces or principles within and it was the crowning fulfillment of the creation sequence. This entity was Man. Here was presented an existence which was similar and dissimilar to nature simultaneously. Man contained within his dimensions something of the higher values of the universal existence and something of the natural rules of the Universe. "And the Lord stated, Man shall be constructed in our *form* and in our *dimensions* (a duplex existence containing Universal spiritual energy and material energy and material existence of the Universe) and thereby he will become master of the fish in the seas, of the fowl in the skies, and of the animals; indeed of all the earth and all 'animal life' which creeps thereupon."

Here in the actual construction we see stated again the principle of the duplex existence. And we see the raison d'etre thereof as the human creative and control instinct over the rest of creation. "And G-d created Man similar to his own existence; he was created in the 'Divine Image" and he was created in male and female mundane existence." The sentence is not to be construed to imply, as superficial thought thereupon may imply, that the human being is an appendage to Divinity. Nothing could be further from the truth. For if it were even remotely likely, we should indeed enjoy a perfect and uninterrupted existence, as was the dream of the Rationalists in the eighteenth century. We cannot reduce Divinity to our conflicts, nor can we raise our conflicts to Divine existence. What the sentence does state is that we, of all existence, are similar to Divine existence in that we possess portions of both higher and lower existence; of universal spirit and Universal matter. In the rest of extant nature there is not present both of these realms which were created on that first introduction of Creation into being. But in us it remains a dichotomy of existence, whereas in divinity it is a unit existence. This duplex existence is summarized in the phrases of human creation; "Divine Image" and "male and female mundane existence." Man is imbued with a passion to create, a divinely attribute, and with natural biological-psychological functions, a mundane attribute. This theme is reiterated in the next chapter of the Bible, which discusses the human existence in greater detail; in this passage: "And the Lord

—G-d formed the Man from 'dust of the ground' (an allusion to his natural qualities) and 'He breathed a spirit of life into his nostrils' (an allusion to his spiritual qualities) and the Man thereupon was set forth as a living creature." And the reason for it all? "And the Lord blessed them, man and woman, and He stated to them 'Be fruitful and multiply and cover the earth' (a blessing similar to that of all creatures created, and added) 'and you shall capture her'," (a blessing stating for man to seek to circumscribe and control the entire natural existence). This is the goal of it all. A little more on this after we have examined that not so glorious existence in the "Garden of Eden."

* * *

Man was presented to the earth and was obliged to sojourn thereupon. There is no reason to suspect that the environment in which he was placed was one in which he would find difficulty in existing. Why should he find more difficulty in adjustment then the other creatures? His was not an "abnormal" existence. Therefore, it is not contrary to one's imagination and reason that the original existential substance of man's environment should be an idyllic and harmonious one. And the Garden of Eden was such a place of sojourn. However, it was not a place of idleness and leisurely relaxation. Man could not have been created just to prove that Man can live in moderate comfort. The Garden was just a calm natural existence in which Man had little discomfort. However, in his spiritual existence, in his creative curiosity, he was advised to have little comfort and much disconcertedness.

The Divine created in the Garden beautiful trees. Of all the trees Man was permitted to consume from the fruits, except one. "The tree which symbolizes the knowledge of good and evil" was placed within the Garden but not allowed to be devoured. Why? What reason had the Divine Creator for causing to be established an entity which Man was not permitted to use? Could it be possible that something was created just to be an Achille's heel to Man's existence? This seems to be the general reasoning which is necessitated according to all those who interpret this Divine Injunction. I disagree, and state that the premise is a false one. It is a misapprehension of the Divine—human being relationship. The Injunction did not disallow the use of the "Tree of Knowledge." It states clearly that man is not allowed to devour or consume from it. You are not permitted to relegate the area of values of good and evil to the natural area of degeneration and generation. You are to deal with the realm of ideas and values with your spiritual adroitness and abilities and not encircle them with natural passions. The realm of ideas was to be used and manipulated by man, by all means. But with the appropriate mental activity and aloof curiosity towards it and not subjecting them to the mundane needs of the human animal. The Universal realm was set upon the Universe and Man was to play therein as long as he used it with the Universal spirit within himself. And on the moment that he would attempt to use his ideas for personal aggrandizement he would suffer death. Death, not physically but spiritually and in his balanced existence. His world was not hostile to him at the outset, nor was it forbidden to him. It was, however, delineated for his own benefit. When he failed to realize this and "ate of the fruit of knowledge" he was forced to suffer the consequences ensuing therefrom. The consequences were that Man would be indeed somewhat outside the realm of nature and outside the realm of spirit. He would see a

Universe which is in its manifold existence quite in harmony and in order. It will work by its normal process of generation and degeneration, construction and destruction. But Man would be incongruous with this existence. The animals will disturb his existence, symbolized by the serpent's hostile attitude for man. The earth itself will not respond to Man anymore, symbolized by the thorny farming necessity of man. And even natural processes within Man will be painful and disturbing to his delicate mentality, symbolized by the labor pains of childbirth.

The world of the spirit will be also little accessible to Man. He will constantly seek to extricate himself from the mire of his natural existence and he will find to his consternation that his spiritual ideals have a distinctly natural covering on them. The distinctiveness of the spiritual world has been lost to Man and he is constantly seeking to discover it. This is quite apart from his given task of creating and controlling the Universe. These tasks are his given prerogatives and he is obliged to seek to fulfill them. But he has another task which was derived from his own blunder, and one which makes him insecure in all his other tasks. That is the task of re-establishing a harmony within his existence between his natural and spiritual forces. So long as he remains in disunity in himself, as he must if he remains in imbalance, he cannot truly control and create.

We see this disrupted harmony in the human being's change in attitude towards his own body. "And they were both naked, the man and his wife, and they were not ashamed of it." They were at that time in no way conscious of themselves or of anything natural. Inhibition, personal and social, could not have developed under these circumstances. After they liberated themselves from their spiritual circumspection, "Their eyes became opened" and they became very self-conscious about themselves and their environment. Already the "Garden of Eden" didn't exist for them anymore. They became wise and felt uncomfortable and self-centered. And they commenced the series of inhibitions which man had to assume in this turbulent situation in order to diminish his over-abundant anxiety. They put dress upon their flesh.

The entire episode concludes with the expulsion of the "Garden" from the Universe. The Universe remains the same, for it was only different in the eyes of the human being. And the Divine states the reason for these divergent natures of the world and of man. "And the Lord-God stated, 'Now the man *was* similar to one of us to be able to comprehend between good and evil.' " He had this ability by token of his having been created from the Universal "Divine Image" portion of the world. We had given him this to use, and he abrogated its privilege by unwisely using his mundane passions in encountering it, and thereby causing a disturbance in his own existence. "And now perhaps he will be inclined to also take with his *hand* of the 'tree of life,' and *devour from it* and therewith gain eternal life." Such an adulterated eternal life would be a catastrophe. He would be an entity which has reached its goal, but who could not enjoy it due to his tormented conflicting heart. We cannot allow man to gain his goal by using his animal-like desires to achieve it. If he wishes eternity he will have to bind his "greedy hand" and his over-abundant emotions and use his spiritual talents to achieve it. And so the "Garden" was closed and guarded by the "Cherubim," a simile for the natural constructive force of nature; and the "glowing ever-turning sword," a simile to the destructive force in nature. This equilibrium was now a challenge and a hindrance to the human being's development of his ideals.

Thus, for Man, to attain eternity he had to right as best possible the chaotic natural—spiritual balance within himself first.

* * *

The episode of the Garden of Eden was not a successful one in the history of man. It was so because man has been given the prerogatives of "free choice." He had an inherent right to choose which path was more to his inclination. This does not mean that he has the choice of avoiding the consequences of his choices. Indeed he has this not at all. And the immediate consequence of his malpractice in his material wants with his spiritual goals was the necessity of assuming additional burdens. These burdens were of two types. On the one hand he no longer felt at ease with his environment, and, on the other, he found it ever more difficult to transact his spiritual needs.

Theologians have been prone to call this episode "the fall" of the human being. In the strict sense that it is used by these theologians, I shall be forced to reject this concept with its attendant interpretation of the story of the Garden. The concept entails that since man has committed a grave transgression of the Divine commandment, he has become beholden to Divinity in such a way as he must redeem himself, so as not to suffer eternal condemnation. This is a basic concept in Christianity and it has been stated by many to be also axiomatically an internal part of Judaism. I cannot disagree too heartily with such a view. This entire concept internalizes a basic statement to which I feel Judaism cannot agree to. Certainly my own reasoning on this statement leads me to reject it as a false comprehension of the Divine intent with his commandments. The statement which must be accepted for one to adhere to "the Fall"

65

concept of man's history is that G-d gave to Adam a commandment which had no purpose attached to it except a will of its Initiator. This means that it was Divinely intended to create a Universe which had a sort of hidden trap in it which man was expressly asked to avoid. Such a statement Judaism has never accepted. There was a Divine commandment and there was also a failure at compliance thereto on the part of man. But the commandment was not a caprice or flaw in creation which man had to avoid, nor was his failure at adhering to this commandment tantamount to eternal damnation. I have already clearly expressed that man was not bidden not to use the "fruit of the Tree of Knowledge" but bidden to use its fruit with those faculties to which it was intended for him to deal in the "orchard of spiritual growth." The commandment was a forewarning to man, implicitly telling him of the reason for it and the consequence which failure at compliance will cause. A commandment is always an aid to the establishment of a stabilization between the natural and spiritual drives in man and to the comprehension thereof. A commandment may take on a prohibitive nature as well as an exhibitive aspect. This does not mean that the prohibition is intended to be a curtailment of the human natural functions. The prohibition curtails over-excessive functioning in one area which will, if unrestrained, cause distortion in the other functions of man. The commandment to Adam was for the avoidance of over-excessive use of his natural functions which would lead to a distortion of his spiritual fulfillment. This he failed to adhere to, as was possible under the circumstances of his freedom of choosing his own set of actions. The result was the consequences which had to be a reaction to his ill-advised action. There was a distortion and a confusion in the fulfillment of both man's natural and

66

his spiritual spheres. Within this confusion he has found it ever more difficult to accomplish the task for which he was created. Yet at times individuals and indeed for certain periods of time whole communities have been able to emerge out of the pathos of human existence and to be creative, and leave a path which others could traverse if diligent enough to emulate.

* * *

This section is written only to pacify those who crave diligently to find the reason for creation, and to show the limitations of inquiry into this field. The answer to the first will demonstrate the second.

Man cannot find the goal in nature. Nature and its equilibrium of action can have no ulterior motive. It cannot state what is accomplished in its incessant movement of diversified functions. Nature can at best be explained to the human mind as means towards an end. The means is not a very docile functioning and certainly demands much attention. But when the analysis thereof reaches into crucial stages one can find nothing more to say about nature except that it is what it is.

Our goal can only be in something which is above nature and not subject to its meaninglessness. It cannot be either ephemeral, or multilateral or contradictory in its fulfillment. It must contain eternalness, unitedness and infiniteness in order to be a destination which will satisfy the human spiritual drive. It is within this context that man seeks to solidify his diversified knowledge and seeks a monolithic substance which is at the foundation of all other knowledge. He seeks therein to establish the identity of the truly unified and infinite existence which is not to be found within

67

nature. He seeks to grasp the eternal fountainhead and to become connected with it.

Only in these terms can we begin to secure insight into the true goals of human existence. The ultimate answer to this question must remain one based upon our experiences and our extant insights. The goal of the human being is to fulfill the potentialities given to him in creation. This is his raison d'etre as indeed it is of the rest of creation. What we can do to extend this statement is only to clarify how and what are man's potentialities and what are his capabilities. From our survey of man's intentions and from a survey of the creation narrative we came to a similar conclusion. That man is the product of two distinct and mutually divergent tendencies; that his need is for fulfillment within both; that this can only be accomplished if he uses his own potentialities in each field correctly; and that it becomes necessary for the maintenance of a complete being for man at times to limit some of his excessive natural drives.

Within this formula, man's amount of possible fulfillment remains manifold. For me to attempt to delimit what areas constitute spiritual success and which segments of existence are for natural accomplishments would be to set finite limits on infinite phenomena. For man has the infinite stretches of all creation to manipulate within. Thus wherever and whenever he touches infinite universality and transcends his own finite existence he is fulfilling his creative abilities. When he lives within his nature and does not become overwhelmed thereby, becoming an animal of drives worse then any other animal, he is also fulfilling his Divinely given attributes. This is the sum total of our explanation of the goal.

It is always possible to find some who will not be satisfied with such an explanation. They ask the question, Why creation? What is the purpose for having created a world with all its responsibilities? To this we must admonish that it is an illicit inquiry. We cannot attempt to comprehend the "Why of Creation." Several important reasons are within the possibility of one to present for this fact. In the first place it is not possible to enlighten thereupon since the Divine has not given us the reason. In the final summation it remains for the Divine to state what his intention is and not for us to impose our various theories, and as far as one can surmise, it has not been revealed. For a second point we must state that we could not possibly apprehend an explanation, for it would necessarily entail an understanding of what is non-creation; or shall we say what did not exist before existence came into being. This is logically beyond our possibilities for we ourselves are part of existence and that which exists cannot understand that which doesn't exist. It is quite analogous to the problem of demonstrating fire to a fish. The fish cannot grasp the concept since he has no possibility of both witnessing fire and remaining alive. We, in our own right, have no possibility of witnessing non-existence and remaining alive. We, however, at times feel that if our spiritual faculties were well used we could answer this question to our contentment and then the above logical impasse would be beyond that which we seek. Here we arrive at still another reason for our inability to respond to the question, why creation. This is that that explanation would entail at least a possibility to transcend our material being. Since this still remains an impracticality, and our material existence would countermand the singleness which such an explanation would imply, we cannot even grasp such a definition of the why of creation, if it were offered. We cannot remain corporeal entities and attempt to deal with non-corporeal ideas at the same instant. The answer in natural terms can only be in relation to fulfillment of function. In spiritual terms it may be more satisfactory, but it cannot be dealt with in these terms while we maintain our natural being which contradicts the spiritual terms of unity.

Someone once explained the task of the philosopher within the analogy of a puppet show. He said that most people see the movement of the puppets, but cannot know how they operate. The philosopher walks around the curtains to the posterior of the show and seeks to uncover and explain the process of how the puppets operate. Why the puppets exist, however, he cannot explicate. This is all that we have been able to accomplish here. The logical impasse is not a small one, and is in my opinion the true reason for the illegality of this question. Even the other reasons at best give possibility for an answer only after one's physical demise from the earth. If that is so then we must be thereto resigned.

We have attempted to bring the world of the Biblical creation tale into comprehension within the terminology of modern man. The reinterpretation of this segment of the Jewish consciousness leads to a concurrence of similar ideas and concepts in both. It also leads, in my opinion, to a more adequate explanation of the meaning of that much perplexing opening section of the Bible.

CHAPTER IV

ENSLAVEMENT AND FREEDOM

Jewish history reached its greatest crisis in the enslavement of the Jews under the Pharoahs thirty-five centuries ago. This episode was a crisis bearing on the conscientious awareness within the entire human race. For it remains within the bounds of necessity for us to discover how it was possible for the human race to develop a civilization whose methods could be so callous as to be described as inhuman. We must also survey this epoch to see its similarities with other historical happenings, past and present. Yet another cause for us to survey this era is to determine how Judaism reacted to this human degradation and what measures of Jewish life are a result of this Galus. The existence of a distinct Jewish religious movement stems from this historical era and the incomprehension of it is tantamount to failure to understand the greater part of Jewish life. One injunction I place upon myself. The explanations will be in line with the theories developed until now. These basic concepts are adequate to give true understanding to this entire phase of Judaism.

* * *

Jacob was in his one hundred and thirtieth year when he left Canaan with his small family group. "With seventy persons your elders departed for Egypt," was stated to the Jews in the Desert. This small group of immigrants were treated rather well upon arrival in Egypt. This was a direct result of their being relatives to the brilliant minister of the Pharaoh, Joseph, son of Jacob. The small band was allowed to sojourn in Goshen which was at this time in all likelihood a distant suburb from the main inhabitation. Here they were allowed to breed cattle and pasture flocks, an act which was not condoned to the native population in Egypt proper. Jacob had failed in several areas to accomplish his life's goals. One could say that the very necessity of living his later years in a land foreign in culture and disposition from his own signifies a lack of accomplishment. In one area, however, he managed to reverse a trait which had predominated in his family all during his life. That trait was the over-abundant rivalry among his many gifted sons. They were constantly seeking not only to outdo each other but to each be the leader over all the rest. Certainly Joseph's outspoken attitudes and the consequent rebuke he received for them from his brothers were only the most extreme examples of a continuing struggle. Still while in Canaan, Jacob had managed to domicile his sons and teach them to live in harmony. When a plight came to Jacob's fortunes we see how all ten elder brothers go together to Egypt to purchase foodstuff, and during the several involved negotiations with Joseph, how they continually arrive at a single counsel of opinion.

When the small clan took journey to the great world center of civilization and commerce, they had been sufficiently orientated by their patriarch's efforts to form a solid and common understanding and unity. The question of leadership was found by the mature men to have been one which was at best negligible, and would, in any event, be in the best interests of all to allow their father to use his discretion in making the choice. The end result was that no one tribe was given any favor by Jacob over the others, except in one instance. That was in the imposition of the two sons of Joseph, Ephraim and Menassah, to an equal status as his own sons maintained. This gave to Joseph's progeny an extra share of inheritance and tribal prestige, which was usually reserved for the first-son; Jacob here indicating that he wished the first-born of Rachel and not of Leah to gain these benefits. It should be well noted that this act by Jacob elicited absolutely no outcries of adverse sympathies on the part of the other sons of Israel; not in Jacob's time nor in any subsequent period. The tribe of Jacob was at last united in fraternal concurrence and would not allow itself to become engulfed again in fraternal rivalries.

*　*　*

Now that we have been introduced to the family of Jacob we must depart from them for a while. This is so, since we must examine what Egypt, the land that they now found themselves in, was like in those days. To give a graphic picture of a civilization long extinct is not the simplest of tasks. This is moreover not truly our inclination. One is most interested in discerning what were the ideals and values of this country; the standards which reflect their weltanschauung and give us means to communicate over a great time break and even greater diversity of existence.

The lower stretches of the Nile River saw the development of one of the earliest and most grandiose civilizations of the ancient world. The geophysical conditions of the area are quite the same ones which exist today. The area is a narrow strip of fertile land which borders on both sides of the river, its fertility due to the regular seasonal overflow of the waters bringing with it a rich deposit of top soil as well as the water, all of which breaks the continuous stretch of north African desert at this point. Within the narrow confines of their geophysical boundaries the Egyptians founded a vast and diversified culture. The remnants of this civilization which we possess today show a great amount of talent in various fields of the arts. They had sculpture and painting, music and dancing, and various types of literary methods. They preserved records individual and state, and they organized large commercial efforts. They were traders with other areas, both by land and by sea. They had accumulated wealth and prestige and luxury beyond that of any recorded previous history.

Yet within their abundant society they had found an unstable tranquility. They could not satiate their need to build physical structures. Their entire spiritual sustenance was found when they were engrossed in the occupation of building. Even before they had completed one scheme for building, they were already busy organizing for a future scheme which would be even more expansive in proportions. This building urge was not a utilitarian urge. The main purpose for their most extensive building projects were for edifices which would serve no use to the living. There was of course rationalization for this extreme building consciousness. It was justified in the myth-legend scheme of the society. This does not detract from the fact that in reality the building program was a mania of the culture.

The result of this mania we observe when we visit Egypt today. The desert is dotted with dozens of pyramids of various different heights. All are almost identical in appearance and serve the same function today as they served when originally built. They served the purpose of harnessing the entire civilization to a colossus project which served no other purpose than the building itself. That they served as graves for the monarchs is no justification for their building, since many monarchs who ruled prior and after the height of the pyramid building era are buried in more conventional graves. We find that many societies have had extreme building drives, usually in the form of majestic palaces or churches. These fulfill, perhaps over-abundantly, both utilitarian, spiritual and aesthetic drives in men. Monuments to the dead are often also grandiose, and these also serve definite benefits to the living; certainly none to the dead. Nowhere do we find an equal to the Egyptian building drives for abodes for the dead.

This pyramid building was only the most glaring manifestation of the social drive. They built palaces to the gods and to the demagogues who ruled the area. They built large grain and storage cities. Their construction schemes were ever more grand and ever more diverse. Over-abundance in economic goods is diverted to some special ideal in any society. In Egypt it was to the ever unfulfilled drive for physical construction.

* * *

The passion of Egypt served another purpose. This purpose was the age old problem of security of the state. It was through this objective that the enslavement of the descendants of Israel was accomplished. "And a new monarch arose in Egypt who was unfamiliar with Joseph; and he stated to his nation, now the people who are descendants of Israel are many and strong within us; let us, therefore, act sagaciously towards this situation, lest they should become overly numerous and should there occur a war, and that nation should decide to join our

75

enemies and engage in battle against us, they would then have the opportunity to leave our land."

The "wisdom of Egypt" was a duplex theory. On the one hand they could decide to help our enemies in any crisis, if they remain in the privileged status that they at present enjoy. On the other hand they could find the possibility to leave Egypt in such a crisis and we would as a result have lost the services of a large group of laborers. This would be detrimental to the national drive of construction. The solution to the dilemma of what to do with this large minority in the country was that they must be harnessed to the national program. They must become integrated to the building zeal of the country.

And so Egypt set about to attain the labors of the Israelites. The Biblical passages do not involve themselves with the process of this achievement. The Midrashim give us many clues that this was not a sudden overthrow of the rights of the Israelites into enslavement. There was a gradual process whereby they were ever to a greater extent bidden to participate in the construction work. The end result was the entire loss of an independent way of life or freedom of choice of objectives and methods by the Israelites. "And they established over it (the Israelite nation) officials to set forth the tasks, thereby to overburden it with work; and they built the stone-storage cities of Pisom and Ramses for the Pharaoh. And the Egyptians compelled the children of Israel to labour relentlessly." The original means towards the end, that of involving the Israelites within the passion of the nation, became an end in itself, whereby it was inconceivable that this minority should be aught but slaves. Their raison d'etre to the Egyptian was to be a slave to his own desires. His overwhelming desire was to see large scale projects abuilding, so that was the area to which they were assigned predominantly.

Thus was achieved the ill-fated situation. It was a combination of the solidarity of the tribes descendant of Jacob and the universal goal of the country in which they dwelt that led to the eventual predicament. The entire group had fallen into the ruse set up for it by the officialdom of Egypt and was now entrapped therein.

* * *

We are now through with the details of the situation. We must now attempt to interpret it into our own conceptual scheme.

This civilization had made, as every one must in our natural circumstances, a balance with life. It was an equilibrium situation which had an outlet for the intense spiritual-creative needs of man. This outlet was, however, not in the realm of spiritual ideals or ideas but in the purely physical-natural world. It was the usage of spiritual quality for natural quantity. It had committed the error of Adam within a large scale setting. It was eating of the fruit of the spiritual heritage of man with the very callous hands of the physical man. This balance was such that only one adversary existed which could disturb it. And that was if there existed a type of life which was different to it. It could not tolerate the presence of a culture which could maintain a way of life which excluded an overwhelming drive to construct. It was intolerant of non-conformity, a fact on which it had no monopoly in history. When it had achieved its unification of natural forces within Egypt to its own scheme, first then was it satisfied.

What the Egyptians failed to realize of their society was that it was entirely enslaved. It was not just the minorities which were enslaved by the majority. The entire civilization was entrapped to its environment and the pattern which it had established. The minority peoples only were subject to a direct physical strait-jacketing from which the main population was exempt. But the mental strait-jacketing which was shared by both, and perhaps even more by the majority, for they were the institutors of the whole pattern, was no less a form of slavery. It was slavery to a harsh taskmaster. That taskmaster was the physical world itself.

Here we arrive at our basic premise. It is that man has only two distinct choices in this world. He can be the master over that world or he can be enslaved therein. When he achieves masterhood over the world then he is free. And when he fails then he must be a slave to the environment. This is the real choice of man. And it is a free choice to which he can determine which path he shall stroll upon. It is when he has made a choice that he must suffer the full consequences of the implications which trail behind the choice. If he determines to live a restricted physical life he will be free to entertain a full spiritual development. If, however, his choice was to immerse his entire self into the vagaries of nature then the consequent results of enforced homage to that nature will result. This full participation in the striving after natural fulfillment leads ultimately to spiritual strangulation of the human being. He becomes worse than an animal, since he must feel the great pangs of forlornness due to the unfulfilled higher drives within him. The overstuffed body is not a satiated one. The Torah states tersely this entire concept towards the end of Deuteronomy. "Behold, I have outlined before you on this day concerning life and goodness, and death and evilness. . . . Let the heavens and earth bare witness to the fact that I have presented to you about life and death, of blessing and debasement; and you should *choose* life in order that you and your seed shall be able to live." The choice is one which each individual must make. When the choice has been dealt with then the results which will incur as a result are not always those which were expected. These will be as direct consequence, however, and should be borne in mind to be imposed if man should *decide* that this path is his. The consequence of immersing one's entire existence into satiation of natural appetite is a loss of freedom. This means an inability to change, modify or initiate new patterns for himself. He must be tied down to the natural order which he has chosen to embrace.

* * *

That the equilibrium which the society of Egypt had assumed could have remained intact is not really questionable. There seems little method to change social equilibriums, especially when they become stratified. From the viewpoint of nature there was no hindrance or modifier to change the life of Egypt from its position.

The spirit of man was not dead by any means yet. The overburdening drive for work was, however, very oppressing to that spirit. It could not revolt, but it could complain. "And it was during those many years that the king of Egypt died, and the children of Israel were overpressed from the labour, and they *cried bitterly,* and their yearnings concerning the labour went up to the Divine." The human spirit was shouting out from its stifled existence for assistance to be liberated. No real words were uttered. No idea was formulated. It was just a deep wail of anxiety and pain under its frustrating oppressor.

Divine intervention was necessary to upset the man made

equilibrium which had been established. It was necessary to upset the society of Egypt in order to liberate the physical, but primarily the spiritual captives of that civilization.

The overthrow of the power of the society came in the form of the ten plagues. These plagues were at once disturbances against the stability of the society and symbols of the impotency of the natural forces which were the idols of Egypt. The first two were directed against the Nile River. This river had of course two natural gifts; water and its marine life. Each one of these was an asset and an idol in the Egyptian system. The plague of *blood* demonstrated that the first asset was less than sure and that of *frogs* showed that the second could be quite disturbing. The next two Divine signs seem to me to be reproaches to the Egyptians' spiritual and physical dependence on the earth and soil. Both the *vermin* and the plague of *mixed beasts* are described in the Torah to have to do with the earth. Of the first it is stated that Aaron would smite the earth to cause their appearance. This seems to be a sign to the impotency or instable character of the fertility nature of earth. If nothing were to grow this would not be seen as a proof of impotency, but the distorted ejection from the earth of vermin was a clear demonstration of the ineptitude of a natural quality at times. The mixed beasts were to plague the homes and "the whole land" of the Egyptians. It was to show the uselessness of the great deal of building which they had striven so greatly to achieve and which used materials from the earth to the greatest extent. The *pestilence* was to degrade the cattle which were assets as food and also worshipped. The *boils* were to show the ineffectualness of health and strength as an ultimate end in man and animals. The *hail* was a demonstration of the vulnerability of plant life in general and the *locusts* to the unreliability of dependence upon the grain crops. The last two plagues were upon the chief nature-gods of ancient Egypt. *Darkness* was an expression of the unreliability for an always regular and inevitable utility of the sun. The *smite of the first-born* was an indication of the falsity of human infallibility; an idea which was ascribed perhaps to all first-born in some measure, but certainly to the ruling monarchs, who were first-born offspring.

Nature is not an end in itself. It is not the omnipotent ruler of the universe. It is not limitless or infallible. It is only the means through which man may reach his goals. It is present for man to be master of and to control. He is given the opportunity to do so, if he but realizes that control entails a sort of non-involved observer type of relationship to nature. This means he must attempt to have an existence in which he will be able to keep his head above the water line of nature. That this is not always accomplished by man we have seen. Can man sustain himself to be able to achieve this goal? Perhaps he can, perhaps not. I think that it was Divine intention for man to achieve this without assistance. It would certainly, from man's point of view, have been a greater achievement if achieved unaided rather than with help. The historical sequences which are related in Genesis are there to reveal that during man's early history only a few individuals had been able to fulfill the means of existence which was intended for them at creation. The duplex constitution of man, natural and spiritual, could not be maintained for the great masses in true coexistence. They fought each other and upset the establishment of tranquil societies. Even if a small group such as Jacob and his family had been able to manifest a satisfactory realization of the true modus vivendi, it was too fragile to sustain them against the greater societies which had not evolved moderate living. This is why when they came into contact with one such a great society as Egypt, their general protective weapon of sojourning apart from the other cultures, was ineffectual to stem the flood of involvement and eventual enslavement. To remain free and prosper, especially as a small nation, they would have to accept Divine assistance. This is the connection of Egypt with Mount Sinai and the acceptance of the Israelites of the Divine commandments through their teacher Moses. In order to sustain a functioning human being and humane society was the Law given, not to act as a series of inhibitions. When viewed through the duplex constitution which man really is, it is seen to be a curtailment in one area in order to be an emancipator in the other. It is to allow man to unleash his great spiritual qualities that we accepted the Torah. And I suspect that those who understood this principle through the many generations since Sinai, and have accepted Torah in this light, have truly been creative instigators and masters of their world.

* * *

Before the Israelites were to depart from Egypt they were instructed concerning this idea. I will outline to the best of my ability how this idea is incorporated in the Torah. The main hazard here is that the concept is expressed in a commandment which composes but one sentence in the Biblical text. The interpretation of the command and the integration with our concepts will occur simultaneously.

"And the Divine stated to Moses and to Aaron while yet in the land of Egypt the following; this month shall be to you the principal month, the first of all the months of the year shall it be for you."

This commandment is the first one offered to the newly liberated nation, while yet not having abandoned the enslaving environs. It is to my mind one of the most difficult of commandments to comprehend. Several queries present themselves to the mind. One immediately wishes to know why this should prove necessary as the first order to the new nation. Its superficial character is that it is only a regulatory measure which could have waited until they were at their homeland or at least until they had evacuated Egypt. What is more puzzling is what nature of command is it? What is injunctioned? It seems to be neither a positive injunction nor a negative one, but only a point of information. No ritual and ceremony or relinquishing of actions is expressed therein. If this is so then the next vexation is what may be the purpose of this law. Surely it must be of greater significance than being a mere indicator of when the start of a new cycle in life commences. It is also to be examined what is the connection of this commandment with the whole concept and organization of the Passover holy days to which it is immediately connected in the Biblical text and in the space of time. An overall difficult task, but I presume not an impossible one.

The reverence and worship for nature and the idolatry connected therewith in the ancient world was a result of the primitive means at man's disposal to control that nature. Man observed the various forms of natural manifestations about him and did not feel comfortable concerning them. He wished to utilize them and control them but he found that this was not always possible. Especially for such large scale phenomena as rain-fall, amount of sunshine, invasion of animal pests against agriculture and pasture, and large scale geo-physical convulsions there was no control and even less comprehension. Man realized that these natural changes were vitally important to the manner of his existence and yet he found that at times nature acted through some strange caprices. There was not too much order or regularity in nature. Only in a few elements did he manage to perceive some regularity. This was particularly in relation to the daily resurgence of the sun after its departure the previous evening. This he felt to be the master over all the rest of nature and he made the sun the highest of his gods. It was the regularity of the sun which lent itself to the imagination as being the controller over the sometimes unanswerable conduct of the other facets of nature. He made of all types of nature an idol, but his greatest idol was the sun god, the god of all the lesser gods.

On the other hand the moon was a very mischievous entity and as such given only small amount of consideration. It had a most mysterious type of movement. It had a habit of appearing and disappearing almost as it desired. To be sure its length of stay was regular, but at times it reappeared in the middle of the day and at times in the middle of the night. Also the number of new moons in a year was not equal to the length of the solar year. There was a strange disparity between the two which could not be justified. No fault could lie with the sun, for it was the master. The fault was with the moon. The whole light and appearance of the moon was feeble and the people could ascribe little controlling power to such an entity. Its mischievous character could only be compared to the activity of love in human beings and generally we find the moon to represent among the ancients the god of love. They have the same incomprehensible character to them.

The emancipation of the Jews entailed that they must no longer concur with the general belief that it was nature who was the ruler of the universe. The ruler of the universe is the non-natural eternal non-vacillating Divinity. The regularity of the sun or any other entity was no proof of its omnipotence. The ten plagues had given sufficient testimony to this effect. Then what took the spiritual place of the departed idolatry? In the Jewish religion it became the acceptance of the Torah, with its dual aspects of recognition of the Divine overlordship in the universe and fulfillment of man's raison d'etre in creation. This revolution in spiritual fulfillment had to be symbolized in every day experience. That symbolization was accomplished by the substitution of the moon and the lunar calendar to a position of importance in Jewish ritual and insignificance for the sun. The symbol of irresponsibility and impotency in the world, the moon and the monthly cycle, was used as a paradigm of all natural impotency. The world is not an end in itself nor a master over the lives of man. It is but the means and material by which he can attain the ends to which he is destined. Added to this is the corollary symbolization that due to this dethronement of nature as master-controller, man is master of his fate. This too is the idea represented by the moon.

With this in view we are able to answer all the questions concerning the commandment "hachodesh." The commandment is a positive institution of a new natural symbol and method to demonstrate the idea of freedom from natural control for man. The symbol is the moon and the month and the method is the determination that this month shall be the initial one in the year. This determining of this period as the initial one serves twin purposes. In the first place it conveys the necessary implication that man does decide concerning nature. Nature itself gives no evidence of having a starting or ending point. It continues in a regular path or cycle without consideration for ought. It shows no favoritism for one period over another. We human beings, however, state that nature has commencement and departure, that certain periods are more significant than others, and that it is man's estimation of various periods which changes them from one meaning to another. This is especially significant in relation to that mysterious movement which we call time. Although we cannot in reality either halt its progress or change its progress, when we assign name and position to time eras, we are in a measure master over it. It is our instituting which will bring certain occurrences in time and not time which will bring certain occurrences to us, as is the theme of astrology. The second purpose of the commandment for setting up this period as the initial one is that it is the corresponding one with the physical and spiritual emancipation of the Israelite nation. It is this significant commencement, which is a type of rebirth or recreation which should be celebrated as the new cycle. It is due to this episode that the Jewish existence has the possibility of being fulfilled. We determine that this shall be the beginning of each period of Jewish life, as it was that first time in Egypt. In practice, because of this the Jews have two New Year days in one year. In Tishrei the new year is celebrated as the commencement of the physical anniversary of the world. In Nison we celebrate, by virtue of this first commandment, the new year of the anniversary of our spiritual recreation.

Now we perceive why this commandment is so important as to be the first issued upon gaining freedom. It is a commandment which gives a symbol for the rationale behind all future commands and rituals. The connection with Passover is also quite clear. This holy day is a period of remembering and reliving the concept of moving from enslavement to freedom. The historical facts do not lie dormant or are not forgotten by the Jews. We incorporate them into the routine of our existence so as to have them as object lessons before us. It is when we forget these lessons that we are necessitated to relive them again in actuality. The Passover in all its details is a simulation of the actual departure of the Israelites from Egypt. Even today our freedom is renewed again each year at this time. We again feel the responsibility of the Torah for attainment of spiritual and physical freedom. That month which contains the Passover within it is indeed the first of months. It is the primary season for the Jewish nation.

The reason for the Mitzvoh of "Kidush Halvanah" (Blessing over the new moon) is connected with this concept. Therein we say "Blessed is your shaper; blessed is your maker; blessed is your master; blessed is your creator." We take the opportunity to reaffirm our faith in the masterhood of the Omnipotent over nature with the advent of the new moon. We state that all of the order and pattern in nature is His Will. We are renouncing nature and affirming Divinity.

There is yet another fact of Jewish law which is connected with this idea. It is not too well known that the dates of Jewish fortunes are determined by imposition by men. The day on which a Jewish holiday is to take place will not be determined by the movement of the days and months, but by the establishment of the calendar by human beings. Of course, to avoid chaos this privilege had to be reserved for a court and it had to function upon certain principles. Yet it remains true that the new month is not started until we announce that it is started. A holiday will fall on such a day and time that we determine due to the manipulation of lengths of months and the number of months in the year. It is precisely this reason that our holidays correspond so negligibly with the solar calendar, which is the predominant calendar in the world. For ulterior motives we may and do change the regularity of the calendar. It is our right to control this and not to be controlled by it.

* * *

To many of the most significant mitzvoth in Judaism is appended the statement that they represent a "remembrance to the evacuation from Egypt." Indeed our entire national-religious existence would not be extant were it not for this evacuation. And this event also gives the reason for many of the subsequent impositions. In the next two chapters I will discuss two areas which stem from this event, one is positive in character the other negative. One thing always is present in Biblical commandments. That is that they counterbalance and work with both sides of life, positive and negative. It is when man has attained a balance of life which does not enslave his spiritual creativeness that he will succeed to a bountiful existence.

CHAPTER V

TUMAH

The human being interacts with nature in two fashions. One is exhibitive and the other is inhibitive. As we have already investigated, the inhibitive attitudes of man to his environment lead to his ability to grow in higher values. Of all the conflicts which man comes into contact with in his lifetime, the greatest for him to resolve is the resolution of the apportionment of his energies to these two different interests satisfactorily. He has the general problem of how much shall he devote of his efforts to practical ends and how much for ideal ends. He faces, moreover, this problem on an almost day to day, item for item decision making basis. He must decide whether a particular act is necessary or could be dispensed with. This decision making becomes very difficult in a society which doesn't have some definite barriers which guide him in making his inhibitive decisions. Such a socety tells him that everything is present for him to use. He is completely free to use whatever, whenever and however he should desire, his entire world. He is told that there is nothing present which may not be utilized at your own whim.

This is quite a pleasant dictum to the ears of man. He forgets his own nature and becomes infatuated by the sweet fruit of nature. And he plunges into the non-restricted nature only to find that he cannot breathe in it. His inhibitive nature requires of him a certain non-indulgence for him to exist. If not he becomes just another over-stuffed cow. What's more the terrible pattern of reaction commences to set in on the participant in nature and he becomes enslaved and enthralled in the constant natural vicissitudes. Man can only become master of the world when he has mastered himself. And mastery of the self entails a distinct policy of separation and limitation of interaction with natural phenomena.

* *_ *

The concept in Judaism which undertakes to limit man's areas of partaking in nature is *Tumah*. It is a word which does not render itself lightly to translation, for being a concept it contains certain implications and rejects others. Its most common translation into English, the word unclean, is quite a false one, although not completely inaccurate. The word in Hebrew comes from a similar stem whose meaning is clogged or filled up. Tumah can best be translated as inaccessible, or impassable. It is applied to those areas where man has been advised not to deal with. There are two antonyms to the word Tumah. One is *Taharah*, which means those areas which are readily accessible and utilizable. The concept is a sort of neutral concept. One can use this realm at will or may not use it. The other antonym is *Kedushah*, or holiness. This is at the other extreme from the first concept. We achieve holiness in objects when we dedicate them to the use of the universal principles of existence, to the ends of Divine Laws. Thus in the mundane world we have assigned three valuation scales to natural phenomena, where only one exists in reality. The two extremes, one for inhibitive purposes and the other for emphasized participatory purposes, have been inserted upon the neutral valuation.

The laws of *Tumah v' Taharah* are very complicated. Many of them have been allowed to lapse into disuse, others haven't any application today. A few Jewish regulations today practiced are, however, based upon them. Principally the laws concerning what foods are permissible for the Jew to eat. There exists an infatuated view among many people that the Jews were very intuitive about sicknesses and the like and therefore restricted upon that basis the use of certain food products. I read once a theory where the Jews were given credit for the prohibition on consumption of hog's meat as a way to prevent trichinosis. Their laws concerning the leper are said to prove that the Jews invented quarantine. Neither statement can be substantiated. The injunctions could not have been health measures, for people didn't comprehend these sicknesses three thousand years ago. If they had been health instructions, there seems to be no reason why we had to wait till comparatively recently for these sicknesses to be universally recognized. These measures, as all those concerning Tumah, are concerned with the spiritual health of the nation, and not with its physical well-being. The physical well-being is sought after in Biblical commands, "and you shall heed diligently your bodies," yet this is only a corollary to spiritual health. We today seek only explanations within physical terms because we have broken our connections with another evaluative measure. That another existed for the Jews in the past, we do not take time out to consider.

Basically this whole area of legislation presents a very difficult problem for modern man. I believe that it was originally instituted to alleviate difficulty in life. I don't feel, as some theologians do, that it could be a purpose of Biblical injunctions to act as a frustrator to life and to see how well man can account for himself in this situation. What I have stated already as my position is that life itself is based upon two contradictory premises. It is the goal of the mitzvoth of the Torah to aid man in achieving an equilibrium of existence in which he will be able to fulfill his destiny. As long as he is continually preoccupied with natural phenomena both physically and mentally he has little means to accomplish all of his destiny. He cannot create in this world when he is always consuming of the natural produce. He must for some moments quit consumption in order to produce something new and creative. Now these restrictive laws present a very difficult problem in themselves to modern man. They can only be operative if man has learned how to create with his mind. They can only be justified as a curtailment of over-indulgence in carnal pleasures which will detract from the possibility of fulfillment in higher values. Man today doesn't even know that there exists another half to himself, other than his physical being. He is unaware that the only way he will ever be satiated will be if he finds a spiritual outlet and slows down his fantastic pace towards ever unfulfilled bodily needs. Not only is he unaware of his spiritual needs, but he is most aware that his appetite seems insatiable. In a slow-moving society, where much labor was necessary to gain a livelihood, there could be the smothering of spiritual needs without the awareness of a lacking. Today man has by his constant efforts to alleviate his work level, achieved a large success in eliminating much labor. The average individual need not work over-bearingly any more. The result is that he has much time on his hands, with which he knows not what to do. He is geared only to a physical world and that world requires less of him than he can give. What shall he do with the rest of himself? This is the real problem of the modern race. What he does do, for he cannot live in a vacuum, is to consume ever greater pleasures. He needs always some new play or entertainment. He spends much of his time roaming about, either on foot or auto, the end result of which is that his time was spent. That it is possible for an individual to spend a useful life on a single word or phrase, is held to be ridiculous. The use of the mind in all its creative power is not possible by most of modern men. He has only his feet with which he roams all over the earth's surface. In such a situation we cannot bid of man to accept restrictions on his participation with nature. He wishes only more participation. He wants to fly to the Moon to alleviate his mental anguish. That it will not be greatly alleviated wherever he physically may venture, he does not realize. He can only be free of the anxiety of life when he fulfills a goal which is outside of nature and perhaps even antithesis to it.

* * *

In the absence of social inhibitors, a community could not exist. How these are initiated and why they should assume certain forms is a matter of much controversy among sociologists, psychologists and historians. It is sufficient to note that every society, in order to function as a group must delimit from the individual's liberty of action. Whether a particular individual is delimited or not depends upon whether he has any desires which are not permissible within the social codes. Social inhibitors are of two types. One is formal or statute and is connected with the state. The other is informal and customary and is connected with social groups. Both offer social pressures on the activities of individuals. Both delimit him in the freedom which he claims is his natural right. What is the universal similarity of all modern study to these restrictors is that there is no way of evaluating them. We say, of course, that it is necessary for them to delimit without too great a confinement of the rights of the individual. This is a laudable statement, but it fails to carry a yardstick with it whereby we can measure if a law is too restrictive or mal-functioning. In the end almost any social system can be justified in some manner. We need not state at length that totalitarian states have been justified even in our own day. It is difficult for one to deny them right of existence and therefore they need little justification on their own.

If we have no criterion to judge the state and society these become ends in themselves. The functioning of the individual is a mere accident which need not be of concern to anyone. It is the dictates of the state and the guiding social pressures which we must constantly watch. If they change direction or motion we must automatically follow suit. If we do not, then we would find ourselves left outside the confines of our directors and we would be floundering directionless. That certain social routine is appropriate for life is not here questionable. But are these ends in themselves? Can we find no other task for the individual but to constantly follow the beams which are pulling at his consciousness to steer in specific directions? It is my humble opinion that the individual must remain the final goal of all existence. Social life is desirable, but the individual's activities as they are potentially possible within his capabilities are the first goals which society should seek to fulfill. If this is so, it does not detract from the necessity of social restriction of the individual. For in his natural needs and demands man is not very individualistic. All people require certain consumption equally and can do without others equally. It is for this reason that the modern techniques of specialization and mass production can be effective. We can produce greatly those items which will be used by almost every individual indiscriminately. We can specialize certain tasks which are not necessary to the individual's fulfillment and thus we can manipulate the task to the criterion of efficiency. Where there is need for individuality we cannot standardize either the product or the task. The individual must forge his own path without much direction. If he had direction he would lose the individual character of the task.

We stated that it is part of man's need to create. This is an individualistic undertaking. Each person will create along lines in which he is capable and has some interests. What will be created is not within the realm of possibility to direct and lead to. We do not know what an individual will next create or whether he will create at all. Most probably the individual himself is unaware how long or great the task may prove to be until he has consummated it. To insure that each individual has the possibility to create in society, should be a criterion as to the worth of social restriction. It may be a good criterion yet it still is no greater a yardstick with which to measure a specific rule's worthiness. For specific rules we are necessitated to accept or not on the basis of some intuitive criteria. This is not very scientific, but we have no choice in the matter.

Now let us return to our own particular restrictors. The laws on Tumah, which contain such a large amount of individual actions within them, are intended to allow the individual to fulfill his creative instincts. How this is accomplished when one eats kosher food is not easily explained. We haven't the yardstick to measure. I myself find it is quite possible for people to become so involved with these laws themselves, in their attainment, that there is little time for creative fulfillment. I was wondering how these laws can fulfill the ideal which, I feel, they are present to help attain, if an individual is unaware of that ideal. It is perplexing to me whether they work sort of automatically, even when one is not aware of it or not. I was also wondering to what extent these laws have to be heeded socially to be of true value. One feels inclined that the greater the universality of adherence to them the more will be their effectiveness, but this is only inclination and in no way that I know of can it be verified.

Of one fact we are certainly aware of. And that is that these laws delimit the amount and the ways of man's participation with nature. Certain areas were set aside which man should not deal with. Certain foods were asked to be not consumed and not touched. Certain objects were asked to be discarded and not used. This reason for social legislation or regulation is not always apparent in modern society. It is always to limit or in some way to set up a balance between the external individual-social conflict of interests. We don't feel that such a conflict exists at all times. In the attainment of higher goals the society should have no say nor any restrictive power. Here the individual should have full power of initiative. In the field of natural wants, however, there must be some inhibition both for social and individual reasons. The amount of these inhibitions should be so as not to delimit the creative abilities of the individual. This is the task of the negative commands of the Torah. If we should ever attain some criteria for evaluation of social phenomena, we may be able to test whether our thesis is justified. Just one last word on this aspect of our discussion. We can't justify a modern custom to any greater extent because of its shorter age or because it is more widely accepted now. This is so because outside ideals influence social norms and direct them and institute them. Of course there are many ideals and many social customs, each of which may be in conflict. There may be social norms which to us at present have no clear attachment to an ideal. But we still favor changes and reforms of social custom on the basis of an ideal, that we have difficulty therein notwithstanding. If this is so the custom which shall predominate will be based on an ideal highly valued. That the customs of Israel and its laws are not widely adhered to among the Jews is that the ideal behind them is not understood and not adhered to. For this reason they become difficult to accept; the reasons for misunderstanding we have already stated. If, however, the ideal which they represent is accepted then the customs which help to attain it will be more readily acceptable.

* * *

The concepts of Tumah are directly connected with the concept of *avodah-zara* (idolatry). "You shall not turn to the idols and you shall not defile yourself with them." Any participation with idolatry leads to defilement. Also a participation and experience of holiness needs a separation from Tumah. "Since I am G-d, your Lord, you shall purify yourselves and remain always holy, for I am Holy, and you should not defile your persons in all the vermin who croach upon the earth." Both the required activity of man and that which is forbidden revolves about the concept of Tumah.

We can comprehend the connection in the light of our thesis of Tumah. We have already in our exposition on the saga of Egypt shown the integral connection of idolatry with the habits of human participation in nature. In reality there are only two choices of religious theocracies. Your divinity must be either outside of all natural phenomena or be part of that natural phenomena. In the Jewish concept of Divinity, there can be no rapprochement between G-d and nature. The one is completely disassociated from the other. Divinity is a unity which is the instigator and director of nature; nature being an entity which in itself presents only a flux of chaotic and haphazard movements.

When a society does not choose to recognize a divinity as being apart from nature, the only remaining choice is to select a divinity in part or all of nature. Only the immature mind can state that it has no religion or no god. Such a statement is a denial of recognition that that individual is led. But each individual must have a director to lead it. It may be that the agent in a particular instance is the individual's own being or mind or personality or whatever, which acts to him as his guide and therefore god. This is certainly a natural god and one of the most obnoxious of idolatries. It could only be accepted by one who has ability to perceive man's capabilities and yet blinds himself from viewing man's limitations.

When a choice of some natural manifestation for divinity is accepted, then there is a circumspection to the power of inhibiting man's passions. This is so for two reasons. The first is that a natural god may be dispossessed and another assumed. It is almost inconceivable of a natural monotheism. In the course of time the natural agent will be found to have some defectiveness or inability which will allow for it to be discarded, or competed with, or to become a symbol for something other than its original purpose. In the second place this agent will suggest through its functioning certain acts as obligatory to maintaining the religious connection. Since this is a natural divinity the practices which will be offered will be certain natural passions. At times these will be exhibited to an extreme and since it is part of the religious ritual, it will not be possible to delimit. Only where the religious concept of divinity is such that G-d is outside of nature and that man's fulfillment is both in natural and spiritual, will it be possible to delimit natural participation by man in any sphere of extant nature.

Thus we can surmise that idolatry will lead to and complement some exaggerated natural passions. We saw this clearly in the civilization of Egypt. Furthermore, many of the prohibitions in the Torah in the area of Tumah and avodah-zara are attributable to similar customs which were advocated by the idolatrous nations about them. The outlawing of idolatry in any of its many forms is prerequisite to accepting a non-natural Divinity. A non-natural Divinity requires moderate participation in nature in order to seek and accomplish with the higher valuative gifts of man. In order to delimit within all the areas of man's activities it is required to dethrone any natural demigods. Thus we complete the circle of reasoning and align all the principal concepts involved. Therefore, idolatry is outlawed so as not to be defiled and also so as to be able to accept the true Divinity. Therefore, Tumah and Kedushah are linked to the historical paradigm of Egypt. "It is since I am G-d who has brought you up from Egypt to be your Lord, that you should remain holy as I myself am Holy." At the termination of the entire sequence of chapters on Tumah and Kedushah in the portion of Kedoshim we are again given the close inter-relatedness of all of these concepts. "And you shall heed all of my injunctions and judgments . . . and you should not walk in the instructs of the nations which I am sending forth from before you. . . . And you shall separate between those animals which you may utilize

(Tahar) and those which you shall hold inaccessible (Tamah). . . . And you shall be holy unto me, as I am Holy, therefore have I separated you out from the nations to be near to me." And upon this conclusion is added immediately the injunction against wizardry and spiritual ritual with dead and bones of dead. The reason for the injunction proceeds its stating. These acts are forms of idolatry of the natural powers of living beings and are to be exterminated from belief and from practice in order to attain a "holy nation."

CHAPTER VI

THE SABBATH

There is one day which is incumbent upon every Jew with which he nevertheless, knows little what to do. He has been taught from very early in life that the chief object of this day is to abstain from doing anything. In one sense, this is a true condition of the day. Yet he is rarely given the other part of the fulfillment of the day. It cannot be, as some may believe, that the entire commemoration of the Sabbath is just to symbolize, with our own forfeiture of work, a Divine act. It is for us to discern what it was that was not accomplished when there was no Divine activity on the seventh day of creation. We must also discern what relation the Sabbath has with the original creation saga and in what light must we act towards the Sabbath.

* * *

To deal with the Sabbath and not discuss the original Biblical text which deals with it, would be an absurdity. We must examine the portion which deals with the seventh day in Bereashith; the portion of the Decalogue which commands adherence to the Sabbath; and the portion which reiterates the Sabbath commandment before the issuance of the second set of the tablets of the Decalogue, in the sedrah *ki sesah*.

"And the heavens and the earth and all their manifestations were complete;" this is the general statement of the termination of the physical and spiritual implementation of creation on the part of the Divine. In the six day period the world had been organized to be of functional value. The functions were completed, but the functioning had not commenced. The use of the world would only commence when the Divine would add some additional feature to the universe. Thus the second statement is, "And the Divine consummated on the seventh day the task which he had accomplished, and He quit on the seventh day from the entire task which he had wrought." This statement is at first sight contradictory in its implications. What was done on the seventh day? We cannot say that nothing was done, for the first half of the sentence states clearly that the task was first consummated on the seventh day of creation. Yet the second half of the same sentence says that that day saw a quitting or resting of the Divine creation, which implies that nothing was done on this day.

The implication of the sentence can be discerned within our frame of reference and indeed it was this inherent concept which led us to use the particular words we did in the translation from the original Hebrew text. At the end of the six days the universe was not complete. It was an organism which was capable of functioning but which had not yet the "breath of life" to commence functioning. It still was directly supported by the Divine Will. It did not maintain movement in time and space independently, which are the characteristics of the functioning universe. Now the Divine Will was to allow the universe to start its functioning before it was "complete." It is as if there is a certain unfulfilled premise in the universe which was there at the end of Divine organization. An area was left open which could serve for creative purposes. An area was left open for man to achieve fulfillment therein.

This is what the sentence states. The seventh day saw the culmination of creation and its commencement into functioning with the quitting on the Divine's Will of a part of its task. The Divine left in universal creation a vacuum which it is the duty of man to seek to fulfill.

We have stated several times that it is part of man's desire and life processes to be a creator of new entities. Such a statement can be a rather presumptuous one. Even if it is our inherent nature to have· such a drive, (as it might be only a false human interpretation of our functions) can we really rise above nature and create? It does seem to be a bit on the impossible side. Certainly within nature itself there is no creation. There is at best, manipulation. Whether this manipulation can become sophisticated enough to allow us to state that one has a control of natural processes is also problematical. As yet we certainly have not reached that point. I have often had occasion to remark that it is impossible for one to view modern technology from a constructive viewpoint alone. As we have perfected the means of construction, so have we simultaneously and ominously counterbalancingly perfected the means to destruction. The atomic age is an era of vast power reactions which can be used almost at will as destructive agents. It takes much more ingenuity to harness these forces to constructive tasks; and the problem of atomic radiation may prove that task to be almost an impossibility. The forces of nature which we are now utilizing are of much greater power potential then those previously used and thus the natural reactions to our usage is much greater. There is much that we can doubt as to man's ability to perfect his dealings with nature so as to control the ill after-effects of every manipulation which we may contrive.

In such a world it seems difficult for man to claim much power for himself, not to mention his being yet an initiator of new objects. Indeed, if the only criterion for such a thesis were our own concepts, we would be forced to assume much doubt and hesitation concerning it. This is not to say that there is no evidence to the contrary. We have attempted to give some such evidence. We would, however, find predicament in the evaluation of our evidence. To assign a value of creation to a particular deed would be quite difficult.

From a religious viewpoint it might be even more presumptuous for us to state that we are assistants to the unfurlment of the world. To place within our own potentialities even a minute fraction of power which is solely attributable to the Divine Infinite Will is quite a brash act. From our own experience it could hardly be justified. We have not been able to attain much infinity or eternity, however much we have perceived them. We haven't much of a yardstick to be able to measure our acts for their accomplishment of higher values and on our own assumptions we could not ascribe for them any such fulfillment.

What we feel to be true, but cannot prove adequately, we can accept with the aid of Divine authority. Such is what the Biblical passages give to us. We are given the statement that the Lord rested or abstained from some Divine act. What does this imply. It must imply that some necessary action was allowed to lay fallow and for someone else to accomplish it. We see that man is created with the Divine inspiration. The whole world of nature does lack something which man possesses. What is more, within that natural world there is no room for creation. Its creation is complete. Where then for man to fulfill the Divine Will to complete creation? We stated that the creation was a duplex one; a physical universe and a spiritual universal existence. If not in the physical world, then in the spiritual realm we can create. And it is our meagre evidence which supports this thesis. Is it not in our world of ideas and thoughts that we have instituted anew? Is it not in our conceptual organization and our metaphysical orientation that we have implemented new ways? Is it not in our perception of the eternal and the perfect that we have managed to extend ourselves into nature and into the universe, where no other natural agent has trodden? We must unite the evidence with the thesis. It is in the unfurlment of the universal principles of existence where man has possibility to discover and create. It is in the implementation of one principle or another to natural existence that man can create and control. And that creation is not manual but mental. It is not physical but spiritual.

* * *

"And the Lord blessed the seventh day and made it holy, for it was on this day that the Lord quit from doing the entire work of creation which He had wrought." There are two words in this sentence which require further elaboration; blessed and holy. The word "blessed" is used in the entire account of the creation to signify that an entity should grow and become more numerous. It is first used on the fifth day in relation to the progeny of the animals of the sea. The amount of water life which existed at the end of creation was not to be the amount which would permanently be established. Each one of the species was to increase in the numbers of its kind so that they will fill the limits of the sea, while the fowl shall be found in all parts of the earth. This blessing is intended to include land animal life also, and therefore no repeat of this is made when the land animals were fashioned on the sixth day. It is next stated in connection with man, and man's blessing is a more complicated one. He is not only given the power of physical multiplication, but also the power of growth in ingenuity so as to be the master of the universe. "And the Lord blessed them, (man and woman) and he stated to them that they should grow and multiply and fill the universe and they shall encompass it." The third mention of "blessed" is in relation to the Sabbath. Here it is coupled with the concept of "holiness." Man is here told that this is a special time for him to grow and to become fulfilled, within a special fashion. It can be accomplished when the growth is connected with the concept and within the realms of *Kedushah*. Kedushah is that part of existence which is a manifestation of the universal portion of existence. It is that type of fulfillment where one uses that human faculty which is in "the likeness of G-d" with which one is created. It is that part of life where the spiritual quality of the human existence is utilized and expressed. It is that part of existence where man creates in the vacuum which the Divine Will has ordained should exist for his benefit. The Sabbath is not meant for man to be a period of stalemate. Quite the contrary, it is to be a period of active growth and achievement. It is to be a time of intense and profound undertaking and fulfillment. But it can only be so if it is correctly perceived and utilized. If one feels that it is a time to rest from the week's activities so as to be able to continue them in the next week, it is a perversion of the concept of the Sabbath. The *Chazal* (Rabbis) always stated and acted with the principle that the whole week's activities were but a means to be able to achieve enough satisfaction so as to be completely free on the Sabbath from mundane activities. We will elaborate upon this point shortly. Thus, the Sabbath is the concept and the imposition of a definite time era for the implementation of the other half of man's growth and fulfillment potentialities. Man is blessed to grow in two ways. One is a physical one, which is in itself more than an animistic fulfillment in that it shall seek to achieve mastery of the entire universe. The other is growth in the metaphysical and spiritual world which is connected with the universal half of creation, connection with which is termed holy.

This is the fundamental concept of the Sabbath. In its later unfurlment it was both broadened in imposition and narrowed in its application. This will not, however, change the fundamental rationale of the Sabbath, but will only moderate the social means of implementation towards the Sabbath.

* * *

The results of the first Sabbath were given to mankind; the Sabbath itself was incorporated into the "way of life" of the children of Israel. "Remind yourself of the Sabbath day and sanctify it," is the fourth commandment within the Decalogue. The sentence, with its two clauses, gives rise to two Halachah concepts. The sanctification of the Sabbath is rendered through the *Kiddush* ritual which is recited upon the first Sabbath meal. The concept of *Zechirah* within the Sabbath has been variously interpreted.

The word—concept *Zechirah* or remembrance does not always signify the same procedure as far as Halachah is concerned.

The commandment that "you should remember the day of your departure from Egypt all the days of your existence" is fulfilled through the mere expression of remembrance.

107

When we state or conjure concerning this epoch in our historical existence then we are fulfilling this command. No further action must be taken to make this remembrance more significant. One must interject here that this statement concerns the fulfillment of this commandment during the entire year and does not deal with the special mode of fulfillment on the Passover.

Another kind of remembrance is that which is connected to a specific positive action. "Be aware of that which Amalek has done to you on the road which you traversed upon your departure from Egypt." Here the injunction demands the fulfillment of the command "to completely obliterate the remembrance of Amalek from under the heavens, never forget this!" The zechirah is to cause the nation to rise above any lethargic tendencies and to accomplish the actions of retribution called for. Thus, remembrance alone is not the fulfillment of this command. Being aware of the past events, without fulfilling the actions necessary and corollary to that awareness, is purposeless.

A third type of remembrance observance within the halachah is that which is present in the commandment of the Sabbath. "The words *heed* and *remember* were stated as one." This rabbinical dictum is stated in relation to the exchange of terminology from the first statement of the Decalogue in Exodus and the second restatement of it in Deuteronomy. What the rabbis are telling us is that the comprehension of the concept involved is only achieved when we integrate the meaning of the two words involved. The remembrance of the Sabbath is complied with only when the Sabbath is adhered to. One cannot maintain that he is fulfilling his obligation to "remember the Sabbath day" by thinking thereof, or reading a passage concerning the Sabbath. We can only remember the Sabbath by consummating the entire set of precepts which are with it connected. This remembrance is also different from that of the commandment on Amalek. There the command to remember and the one to destroy Amalek are each separate ordinances. Each one states a separate phase of the task to achieve its culmination. In the Sabbath law there are not two separate *mitzvoth,* but only one. When one diligently accomplishes the rules of the Sabbath, he is remembering it. And when one wishes to remember the Sabbath, he must adhere to it in order to do so.

There is found in rabbinic literature another interpretation to the word *remember* in the Sabbath command. This interpretation is not one which is approved as within the meaning of the actual statute, and the procedural actions which are therein implied are not obligatory. It is most interesting to the controversy of Hillel and Shammai concerning it. Rashi quotes a *Gemarah* in the tractite *Baitzah* in his commentary on the command of the Sabbath in the Decalogue. "Give heart to continuously remind yourself of the Sabbath, so that if a beautiful object comes into your possession, keep it for use on the Sabbath." Nachmanides (the Ramban) comments upon this piece of Rashi and brings the full text of a Mechilta, where the same is stated. He says that it is not an obligatory *halachah,* which we deduce from the controversy of Hillel and Shammai. He quotes, "It was thusly learned: they related concerning the habit of Shammai, the elder, that all his life he 'ate' for the Sabbath. How did he accomplish this? He would locate a worthy animal and set it aside for the honor of the Sabbath. If, on the following day, he would encounter an animal of greater value than the one he was keeping, he set this second one aside for the Sabbath and consumed the first one. However, Hillel, the elder, had a differing habit.

All of his duties were done for the 'heavenly glory' as the sentence, which he often quoted, states "Blessed is the L-rd, each day He assists us."

Some explanation is necessary for us to be able to comprehend the difference of opinion between these two giants of Jewish thought. What seems apparent from a first glance at the above quoted section is that there is a failure to clash between the two statements. Shammai's custom is a specific one relating to the Sabbath and Hillel's is referring to all the acts of life. Furthermore, from the statement of Hillel's mode, we might infer that Shammai, contrary to him, did not execute all of his deeds for the "heavenly glory." This could not be the intent or meaning of the passage. We are not being told that one was more pious than the other. There is a fundamental difference in the method and attitude to fulfilling the Sabbath commandment involved. Also there is a difference in their attitudes towards the fulfillment of the religious goals of man.

We find in Jewish history very often where a person will take a specific *mitzvah* and emphasize it within his personal life. Not that he does only this one *mitzvah* at the expense of others, but he will fulfill the obligations of the others as is required and will practice this one *mitzvah* "beyond the boundaries of the required law." This is, in fact, one of the symptoms, if you will, of a truly pious Jew. We know, for instance, that Hillel overemphasized the *mitzvah* of "peace in the family" or harmonious personal relationships. It is said, "Hillel would advise: be of the students of Aaron; love harmony and run after harmony." This was his special duty and one which he gave special attention to. Shammai's *mitzvah* for special attention was the Sabbath. He put the whole resources of his being into fulfilling this commandment to its finest. We know that a part of the *mitzvah* is *Ta'anug* or pleasurable circumstances. This is so that one will have no deprivations on the Sabbath and will feel most comfortable, so as to have very little mental and physical anxiety. Shammai made it his duty to put great efforts into fulfilling this concept. As we see from the *Mechilta*, he would consume during the whole week in relation to the Sabbath. All of his possessions and their utilization were organized so that he would have the finest things ready for the Sabbath. Shammai is the paradigm in Jewish history for the complete and beyond the call of duty fulfillment of the Sabbath.

Now these activities in themselves were not an end in themselves. They were accomplished so that the Sabbath would be well observed. The observance of the Sabbath was the end which was sought by Shammai. This observance of the fulfillment of the human creation within the limits of that potential creativity was the object of Shammai's intents. He sought to sanctify the Sabbath in a material sense as well as a spiritual one, to be able to obtain a perfectly harmonious environment in which to best negotiate the Sabbath activities.

Hillel did not argue apropos this custom of Shammai. He could not state that it was an undesirable mode, since it was surely a very appropriate one. Hillel had a different mode of life, however. We can discern from his habit that he had some disagreement with Shammai. Basically, he felt that however great Shammai's acts were in relation to the Sabbath, their scope was somewhat limited. We can discern two different objections which Hillel had to this practice. First of all, he felt that this dedication of material and organization to the Sabbath, and thereby to G-d, was limited. There are many situations which occur in man's existence which cannot be put aside until the Sabbath day and then utilized for the Divine purpose. There are many situations which occur momentarily and suddenly. These things must also be utilized for the "heavenly glory." Thus he said that we should do *all* of our activities for the glorification and fulfillment of the Divine purpose in the universe. What you do, Shammai, is most admirable, but it certainly is not enough. It does not deal with all the activities of man. This is the diversity between Hillel and Shammai on the fulfillment of the religious goal of man with the Sabbath. In this context the sentence which Hillel would always state, "Blessed is the L-rd, each day He assists us," means that there are many daily activities which manifest His everpresence and His constant aid and our dependence thereupon.

Hillel had still another objection to Shammai's practice. This is a difference in the rationale of the fulfillment of the Sabbath itself. Hillel felt that the goals of the Sabbath were not meant to be utilized on the Sabbath alone, but on every day and in every act. The Sabbath day itself is just a special time set aside as a remembrance of the first Sabbath and a time when we can condition ourselves to act spiritually. But the spiritual activities of man are not relegated to the Sabbath itself. We must seek always to make our spiritual capacities predominate over our mundane existence. Thus what Shammai did in preoccupying himself with organization for the Sabbath day itself is at best only one facet of the situation. We must also organize our assets which we gain on the Sabbath and utilize them during the whole week. We must attempt to bring about in our lives the concept which the Chazal called "an era when all is as the Sabbath" (*Yom shekulo Shabbos*). Thus when he said that we must do all of our activities for the "heavenly glory" he was stating that we should do so at all times and not only on the Sabbath. Always we must activate our spiritual heritage and potential to the fullest of our abilities. And the sentence which he quoted means that the Divine is present each and every day and that due to His will or assistance, we can fulfill our raison d'etre on every day and in every act of our lives. The Sabbath is the paradigm and the compulsory, but we must augment its meaning to the rest of the week.

* * *

"For six days you shall labor and accomplish all of your work, and on the seventh day it shall be a Sabbath to the L-rd, your G-d, you shall not do any work."

How do we know what manner of task is one to be called work and not to be done on the Sabbath? Only one specific task is stated in the Torah. That is the admonition against the using of fire on the Sabbath. The other classes of chores which are not permissible to be done on the Sabbath are derived from the tasks done in the *mishcan* (the temporary tabernacle of the desert in Sinai). The sages organized from the differing types of chores that were done in the *mishcan* thirty-nine principal categories of "work."

The perplexity which presents itself concerning this is that these categories of work were not outlawed in the *mishcan* or later in the Temple. The tasks which are generally outlawed on the Sabbath were carried out in the *mishcan* itself on the Sabbath. They had to be done in order to bring the communal sacrifices. Of course, personal sacrifices were not brought or used on the Sabbath. Yet even the limited extent to which these tasks were in the "center of Jewish life" accomplished on the Sabbath presents the following problem. How can we derive the content of the outlawed tasks for the Sabbath from a context in which they

113

are at all times, including the Sabbath, permitted? How can we compare the two areas, the general and the particular and then derive contradictory consequences? And if these tasks are outlawed on the Sabbath, how can we profane the Sabbath in the holiest area of the community?

The answer is that what is done in the tabernacle or the Temple is not "work." It is only that from this we can derive what is work, but not that this constitutes a job. One of the basic concepts in determining what we mean by work in the Sabbath is the halachic precept "The thought was what the Torah prohibited." It is not the actual task which is done by which we measure whether a type of work is done. It is by the thought behind the task, the intent of the doer, with which we can establish if a task is done. A chore is termed work if it is done for the person's own bodily satisfaction. Something which is done for a religious reason is not called a chore. But this one criterion is not enough. We need something else besides the rule of intent. We need some specific categories of what is work in order to delimit what can be done and what cannot be done. For if we don't know that, we would have to say that absolutely nothing is permissible on the Sabbath; not even rising from one's bed, as this is for a personal satisfaction. These categories we derive from the *mishcan*. This is so because what was therein done represents all types of chores done by man. This is because the concept of sacrifice is to give a part of one's self to G-d both materially and physically. Therefore a sacrifice will represent in the material all the main consumptive materials of the community. These duties in the *mishcan* therefore, represent the work done in the community. Therefore, they are appropriate as categories of work. But we must remember they are only termed work when they are done in the regular course of events in the community, while when carried on in the sacrificial order they are not done for any directly personal reasons and therefore are not work. This is the reason why only communal sacrifices are burned on the Sabbath. Individually brought sacrifices certainly fulfill personal satisfaction and this would make the tasks therein entailed called "work."

* * *

Prior to the reissuance of the tablets of the Decalogue, there was a restatement of the Sabbath command. "And the L-rd told Moses the following, and you relate to the children of Israel thusly: Only heed diligently the Sabbath; for it is a symbol for all generations between Me and you to demonstrate that it is I who made you holy!"

Here the word "only" (ach) presents a problem which must be dealt with. It is a diminutive which deflates the concept which will be discussed immediately after. In this case it diminishes the concept of the Sabbath. This means that we can accomplish the Sabbath in a decreased fashion from its original institution. We can keep the Sabbath, by heeding diligently to all of its precepts and establishing it as a symbol of the recognition on our part of G-d as the creator of man. This recognition is to contemplate that all of the capabilities of the human being to be a spiritual entity and perceive holiness is due to the fashion in which the L-rd created us. Thus, to heed the Sabbath and to remember through its symbolization the Creator is the least that must be done by the Jew. "Only" remember this should be at least always accomplished. Of course there is much that can be done on the Sabbath. But "the day is short and the work great, and the person is very lethargic." This should not call for a complete abandoning of the

Sabbath. We would fill the vacuum with mundane pleasures. At least heed the Sabbath well and create the vacuum in the week's activities, to remind yourself that, how ill you can accomplish with it, you do possess another side to your existence. This is what the L-rd asked, and which Jews have for thousands of years attempted to comply with.

The Sabbath is thus pictured as being many faceted. The basic premise is, however, that it is principally a positive command and one in which much is to be done. If this is not always seen within the large amount of inhibition within the Sabbath observance, this is because the negative side is more easily accomplished and more paramount for the survival of the entire concept.

CHAPTER VII

THE SACRIFICE OF THE SELF

The several different themes which we have till now discussed are, within our initial context, universals with a "Jewish dress" to them. We have attempted to demonstrate their relationship to the whole life pattern of the human being. This is in contrast to the recent, "modern students" of religion who tend to find no other explanation for religious precepts, except certain socio-cultural goals. This usually does not help to explicate any religion at all, but only attempts to show the relatedness between various religions and religious feelings in the human being. What form these feelings assume we know only by empirical investigation and documentation. We have tried to give perspective to religion within the entire cosmic existence of man and not identified it with just a part of his emotional repertoire.

This chapter and the one to follow it will deal with two concepts which are almost exclusive to the Jewish religious spirit. It is not in their existence that they are exclusively present to Judaism, but in the extreme form in which they are practiced in her. Each of these concepts form a basic departure of the Jewish people from that of their neighbors in relation to a principal religious act and emotion. We will attempt to outline the primary Biblical—historical events which are paradigms of these religious concepts. However, one should be reminded that they have been experienced again and again in every generation since the first Jew, Abraham, began his wanderings upon this earth. With only slight alteration of dates and names, the events which took place several thousand years ago may be paralleled to ones which occurred in the twentieth century.

* * *

We shall commence with the concept of sacrifice, which is certainly one of the foundations of all religious feeling. The sacrifice and ceremonies surrounding it are found in all religions of antiquity. Only the comparatively modern western religious creeds have found it possible to relieve themselves of the burden of sacrifices. How this has been possible we will later attempt to theorize upon. But even within the western creeds there is usually a symbolization of sacrifice and there exists within the liturgy constant reminders of primeval sacrificial events.

What is a sacrifice? It seems that the only thing which enters our imaginations when we think of a sacrifice is that it is some abhorrent ceremony which is very inhumane and anyway old-fashioned. Why it should be so objectionable to modern man seems to me to be a perplexity. It is, within his own civilization, a most irrational objection. Not only does he slaughter for personal consumption millions of animals each year, but he also has slaughtered millions of human beings for his own passions and intrigues. I wonder how many of the millions of humanists who cannot hear of animal sacrifice were at all disturbed over the millions of human beings who were exterminated with the flick of a gas switch? I wonder still more how many people remember today this grotesque event which occurred so recently in our own lives, and for which we all are to a great extent still guilty? (I include in the pronoun even the Jews and nations who suffered most under the maniacal tyranny which over-ran western civilization just one short decade ago. In an era when we have moved so far in controlling the course of unbridled nature, we have simultaneously unleashed the most reprehensible of facets to the human nature. Until we learn that control of ourselves is of prime importance, we will not have absolved ourselves, by learning from the events which we lived through, from the crimes against humanity of Nazi Germany.) I would also like to ask persons who find only abhorrence in mentioning animal slaughter, whether it would not be perhaps worthwhile to have animal slaughter in order to redeem individuals from suffering such a fate? I would not personally state whether such a possibility exists or should be instituted. Whether sacrifices will ever reenter into practice in any western religion, including Judaism, is very questionable. The circumstances for such an undertaking are not now present. Yet we should not as a result think it either impossible or abhorrent. If we can bring such large quantities of resources to the altar of man's egoistic passions, can we find none for the awakening of the spiritual heritage of the human race?

* * *

We return to our original question, What is a sacrifice? To answer this question we must turn our attention to the first sacrifice recorded in history. That sacrifice was the one brought by the two sons of Adam, Cain and Abel. It is their example which will set the way for future sacrificial ceremonies and which will give us the clues with which to describe the significance of the sacrifice to man.

It was after the expulsion from Eden that Adam had a family. The eldest son Cain was a farmer while his younger brother chose to be a shepherd. "And it occurred after the elapse of some time, that Cain brought from the fruit of his lands a present unto the L-rd. And Abel also brought from the first fruits of his herd and from the choicest parts thereof; and the L-rd found favor in Abel and in his offering. And with Cain and with his offering no favor was shown; whereupon Cain became exceedingly angry and crestfallen."

This is the related occurrence. Why it was that the Divine chose the one sacrifice and not the other is apparently not revealed. From the account of the offerings we can discern no ulterior motive for the choice of the one and the rejection of the other. There are those who subscribe to the "rotten apples" theory in stating that Cain brought not of the best fruit in his offering. There seems no reason to suspect that this could have been an important factor in the difference in the twin offerings. If the fruits were not of the best ones, as a *Midrash* points out, then what is significant is to discover the reason why the presenter used these articles in preference to others. The Divine decision to recognize one's present in deference to the other is due to something rotten in the individual and not in the fruit. The mode of presentation is only symptomatic of the disease. Thus we must find the point of departure of the two sacrifices in the individuals who offered them. Of our own accord we find no hint to the differences between Cain and Abel. The several sentences in the Bible offer too meagre a description of these persons for us to be able to distinguish some fundamental psychic difference. Only from the immediate conversation which the Divine had with Cain concerning his disappointment over his efforts can we extract a concept for the reason of the Divine rejection. And with this concept we will be able to discover what were the superlative qualities of Abel's sacrifice.

This conversation contains a sentence which is one of

the very difficult ones of the entire Chumash. We will here present our views while keeping in mind that at each point of the way several alternative explanations present themselves, and that we have chosen those which give best credence to the entire topic and afford the best means of obtaining an objective insight into the affair.

"And the L-rd said to Cain: Why are you so angered and why should you be so crestfallen? Now if you had done well, it would certainly have been accepted; but if you had done improperly, the sin is lying at your door; and it thusly impels you, whereas you should be master over it."

What has the L-rd told Cain about his offering? He is told that the sacrifice was not a good one because you have chosen to seek the sacrifice as a means of personal fulfillment and wish recognition thereof. The sacrifice cannot be accepted because you have attached your own wishes to it. This is the meaning of the words "the sin is lying at your door." The second half of the statement admonishes Cain of the consequences which will result from this attitude. Since he has sought through the sacrifice to find fulfillment and recognition, it has been a failure; and since it has been a failure he has lacked his intended fulfillment. Thus he feels insatiated and there is a void in his needs which forces him into action and compels him into mischief. As a result his psychic is propelling him, whereas he should be master of his passions. It is this awful impulsion which has resulted from your type of sacrifice, Cain. And it is this uncontrolled state which leads you on to wrath and to humiliation; and from there on to the terrible act of fraternal assassination.

What then is the difference in the two sacrifices brought by the sons of Adam? The one brought by the elder son was brought for his personal needs. It was brought with full recognition of the Divine and his authority. Yet it was not a sacrifice of the individual, by any manner or means. It was only the taking of one part of the produce of the individual and using it as means of gratiating the L-rd and thereby seeking favor in his eyes. What would this favor entail? It would entail at least some divine "pat on the back," but usually entails the hope that the Divine will look well upon the individual in his future endeavors. There is a distinct reason behind the offering. There is no doubt as to what the producer seeks. It is his wish to have the vicissitudes of his future existence minimized and even expelled as a reward for his showing recognition and giving of himself to the Divine. The sacrifice remains his own and is intended to be compensated for; reciprocated in some benefit which is within his wishes.

This is only the one type of sacrifice. There exists another type which is quite different from the first. In this sacrifice the person who offers it partakes in it perhaps to a greater degree than is found in the first type of sacrifice. Yet his participation and particularly his expectations from the event are quite different. In this sacrifice the individual brings the offering only as a means of showing that he recognizes and is aware of the presence of his L-rd. No ulterior motive is injected into the presentation. No special favor or grant is requested, nor is any expected. The main aspect of this sacrifice is that no reason or reasoning lies behind it. Neither is it a Divine request nor a human imperative. It is neither rational nor meta-rational; and one doubts if an emotional benefit or desire is involved. It has, in a word, no purpose. It is a result of the fact that man is alive and that part of being a human being seems to be to find it possible to give of oneself to something outside and completely disassociated from his own existence. It is the utilization of some part of the man's abilities for an area completely separated from his own known wants and cares and thus cannot be in any way said to have a purpose. This is what is meant by the "total sacrifice." It is one which is done knowingly and with full intention of being only a sacrifice. What will occur in the future, or what did happen in the past should in no way influence or be influenced thereby. It is not accomplished for any pleasurable benefits. Such is the sacrifice which was brought by Abel to his L-rd. It was the giving of some part of his efforts to the Divine, with no intention of getting a return reward for it. It was not a means towards some other end. It was an end in itself; an end which sought no additional objectives.

This then is the answer to our quest for understanding what a sacrifice is. It is not a simple, but a duplex category. One part is that which is similar to all other types of human activity in that it seeks some additional or constructive benefit for the performance of the rites. The other is the total act of sacrifice as an event in itself, for itself and without consideration of other events. It is this second type of sacrifice which has found favor in the L-rd's eye as the saga of Cain and Abel reveals. And it was the throwback of the sacrifice to himself which was "rotten" and which was unappreciated in the act. It was not the total, unadulterated commitment of a part of the self for the Divine presence.

* * *

This fundamental attitude towards the sacrifice has been incorporated in Judaism and has been slightly augmented. The paramount instance of human sacrifice in Jewish history is the sacrifice of Isaac on the "Akedah" by his father Abraham. Here we witness the total sacrifice to the L-rd not only with a part of one's life but with the entire life. The narrative in Genesis of this episode is quite clear.

There is no motive given by the Divine for requesting of Abraham to bring his most beloved son upon the altar. And the great fulfillment of the commandment is that neither father nor son belittle the sacrifice through asking what purpose it shall serve. What is even more significant to be noted is that with the sacrifice of Isaac the promises of the L-rd to Abraham would be unfulfillable. For it was many years before, at the expulsion of Hagar and her son Ishmael from the house of Abraham that the L-rd stated that "only through Isaac shall your progeny be recalled." This fact was again restipulated when the L-rd commanded Abraham to bring his son for a sacrifice, as it is written, "And He said, take your son, your singular one, the one you love dearly, Isaac and bring him up as an *Olah* on one of the heights which I shall advise you about." Isaac is here detailed as the single son or special son of the children of Abraham. And it was from his descendants that the promises of the Divine should be fulfilled. Thus, when the sacrifice of Isaac's life is requested it should occur to one to inquire what would result with the outstanding promises of the L-rd? This was not asked and was a non-consequential question. Whatever the L-rd should choose to do to honor or perhaps abrogate his obligations are of no concern with the immediate injunction. The sacrifice has been appealed for and it must without any delays or qualms of questioning be executed.

The sacrifice was in all events completed. Although Isaac was not himself cut off from life, as the original commandment had stated, he was sacrificed. This was accomplished when the ram which had been caught by its horns in a bush nearby, was placed upon the altar in Isaac's stead. The actual physical sacrifice was that of the ram. But the physical bringing of the ram to the altar was only a symbol of the sacrifice of the man. When the father drew the knife across the neck of the ram he felt that this is as if my son were being sacrificed to the L-rd. So also was the thought of the son. This animal is symbolic of my own sacrifice, total and complete, to the L-rd. This is the reason why the ram had to be placed on the altar after the L-rd had found that Abraham had completed His wishes and fulfilled His command. That is also what is intended by the sentence in the Torah which reads, "And Abraham stepped forward and took hold of the ram, and he placed it up for an Olah *instead* of his son." It was a symbolic procedure instead of his son's actual sacrifice. But in the minds of the two, father and son, it was as if the person himself had been sacrificed; and it was with this that they did execute altogether the original divine command.

* * *

The next important incorporation of this concept was in the *karban pesach* which was commanded immediately prior to the departure of the Jews from Egypt. Immediately after the singular command of the establishing of that month of their departure as the first one of the year, they were commanded upon this sacrifice. It is a very different type of sacrifice than any which was previously or subsequently reported in the Bible. Undoubtedly some of its essentials were due to the link between this sacrifice and the last of the ten plagues, the blight on all the first-born children. Herein is symbolized the consequences of the two different systems; one a natural practical dependency, and the other a supernatural illogical personal sacrifice. The former leads to an inevitable destruction of its most vociferous adherents to compensate for its overactive grandiose construction schemes. The latter leads to an individual and personal freedom and an internal security in the face of adversity.

125

That is the reason why the blood of the *pesach* was placed upon the two doorposts to signify an Israelite family and to save its first-born from destruction.

The other element of this sacrifice is that it is the complete sacrifice of the individual through the symbolization of the sacrificial animal. Let us examine the principal regulations regarding the bringing of this sacrifice. "And you shall eat the meat on this night roasted on fire, together with matzah and bitter herbs. You shall not eat of it half-done, nor cooked in water, but only roasted on fire, the head with the feet and the innards. And you shall not leave over of it until the next morning, and what shall remain till near the morning should be scorched in fire." This is the only sacrifice which requires that it be roasted thoroughly before one can eat from it. This is so that there should not be any substantial gratification as a result of consuming this animal. The animal's consumption is to be only a substitute and a sign of the individual's own sacrifice to the L-rd at the moment of his greatest triumph, his gaining his freedom from his oppression. This is also the reason why the devouring of the Pesach requires that matzah and marror (bitter herbs) be eaten alongside. These two food items are rather paltry in their value as nutritional substances and are rather substantially ill-palatable to the great majority of people. They add immensely to the non-pleasurable aspect of the pesach and aid in the attaining of the concept that this entire procedure is to make the individual feel that he himself is being offered to the Divine. For this very same reason the Torah forbade the breaking of a bone in the karban pesach. This is so since the bones could not be well roasted and if they were broken while eating there may accrue some especially fine taste from the marrow of the bones. Since this sacrifice is to symbolize the complete surrendering of the self upon the altar, this would be a profanation of its intent, and therefore we abjure from allowance of the breaking of any bones in this sacrifice. The last injunction of significance concerning the procedure of eating the pesach is that it must be completely eaten, with no flesh left over until the following morning. The prohibition is declared in order that the completeness of the sacrifice shall be established. It is to be a total sacrifice that the human being is giving and demonstrating in the pesach, and to leave over from the original would mean a less than total sacrifice. It is for this reason that it was required to calculate previously how many persons would be necessary to consume one animal and to assign every individual to a specific household, according to how many people were present there and according to how much each person therein could consume. If at all possible it was necessary to attempt to have the animal completely consumed on the night of liberation. Only if some meat was left over, then it was to be burned in order to have the completeness of the sacrifice remain intact. But this was only an emergency measure, since the best fulfillment of the sacrifice was where it was both complete and devoured by the household. In this case the Israelites felt the bitterness and toughness and charredness of the meat, and could account that it was as if they themselves had been put upon an altar; and they would have the total extinction of the animal which would be seen as if their own personal sacrifice were also a total, all-surrendering action.

This then is the *karban pesach*. It is the entire nation's equivalent to the individuals Abraham and Isaac's sacrifice. Besides the institution of a pesach to be brought subsequently every year on the day before Passover, there was also established in the repertoire of sacrifices the special type known as the "olah." This is a sacrifice similar to that which was brought by the patriarchs. It is in contrast to other present offerings or sin offerings brought in the temple, in that no part of it is ever eaten. In the other types some parts are either given to the *cohen* or they are to be eaten by him and his family; or sometimes to be consumed partly by the Israelite who brings the sacrifice; each type of sacrifice having its own regulations, with only part of the entire animal being brought upon the altar. The olah however, is entirely burnt upon the altar and no part of it is eaten by anyone. It is the sacrifice which can be brought by an individual who wishes to demonstrate that he comprehends and acts according to the concept that it is part of the fulfillment of the human being to be willing and able to give himself entirely over to an end which entails no personal gain. This is the type of sacrifice which is the preferred one, if not the only real one. This sacrifice is at the heart of so much of what is Jewish and of so much of what is ill-comprehended in Judaism.

* * *

In this same vein is the famous mishnah of Antignos in the tract called *Abot*. Let us quote this mishnah. "He, Antignos, was wont to state, do not emulate those servants who serve their masters in order to gain a reward; however, be as those servants who serve their masters with no intention of gaining a reward, and the 'fear of heaven' should be upon you."

Antignos addressed this principle to his students. It was not accepted by all of them and was particularly misunderstood by two men, Zadok and Beisus, who not only revolted against their teacher as a consequence, but also formed a group to oppose the Antignosian teaching, as they had construed it. These two men had understood that the propounder was denying the existence of any sort of reward to one who acts in a righteous fashion. They claimed that many Biblical passages showed quite the contrary to be the Jewish view. And generally speaking, there is no denying that many Biblical and Talmudical passages stipulate a reward for righteous deeds. There is much controversy concerning the details of the rewards and their allotment, differences being based on varying metaphysical concepts, the details of which it would be hazardous and difficult for us to here dwell upon.

A close examination of Antignos' words will indicate that he was falsely interpreted by his overimaginative students. His principle is of itself quite difficult to comprehend when viewed in isolation. The metaphoric impression hides the actual intent. Yet when it is seen in the light of the concept which we have previously herein delineated, then one will observe almost immediately the similarity and close connection between the two.

I will use the impressive commentary of Don Isaac Abrabanal, instead of my own words, to depict the meaning of the teacher. "And so the pious Antignos admonishes man, that his labours should not constitute that type which hopes for a reward in the future or who has fear of the future punishment which will accrue, but he shall be of that concept which conjures that it is an obligation upon him that he accepts the Almighty and that he does this labour." It is not part of Antignos' instruction that there is no reward. He is concerned with the mode of serving the Divine. His principle is that principle which has always been the Jewish attitude to sacrifice. He only enlarges it to cover the entire realm of man's serving the L-rd; for in everyone of the services to the Divine there exists a certain sacrifice on the part of man. In every case the individual who wishes to perform the act in accordance with its underlying principle must realize that the fulfillment of the act will only arise when it is executed as a total sacrifice. This is the method of serving the L-rd which is the most profound. Whatever reward or otherwise that should accrue due to the enactment of a certain *mitzvah* is not to be considered, nor is it consequential, to the *mitzvah*. This is true whether the betterment which should be reaped is one which is handed out in this life or in the world to come. Whatever the relationship in the logical position of ethical living and rewards for it, it remains immaterial to the doing of the specific command. Indeed it is quite impossible for us to deduce the causal connections between specific acts and their rewards in the field of ethics. Even a broad theory of ethics which is based on a pragmatic or functionalist viewpoint cannot at all substantiate the necessity for moral living. This is because it is almost impossible to measure the results of moral living and to find out in an empirical situation that this is better then living amorally or unethically. In the end ethical living is one of those human methods which man has assumed, and under most circumstances it remains a physical burden. Maimonides expresses the viewpoint in relation to rewards for services, that these are necessarily a weapon for aiding adherence to the commandments, and uses the simile of the child's receiving a sweet reward upon acting according to instruction. We who dole out the candy to the child realize that it is not for the purpose of receiving the candy that we wish the child to act in a specific fashion, but the child does not thusly realize. However, as it matures it will realize that the rewards are only our way of coaxing it to walk upon a straight path, and then it will no longer require of us the reward in order to act justly or wisely. So too is the case with the rewards which are expressed in Biblical passages. This is an explanation which will serve us well, although we need not accept it as the only clear alternative. Even this statement shows the almost rigid law of not binding the act with the reward or punishment. In the judicial process, where men must associate the act with ultimate retribution, we assign rewards and punishments. But these are not always a direct logical result of the act; they are influenced by other considerations than the mere execution of some act or transgression. Furthermore, even in this process we have occasion to find where an illegal act will not incur a punishment. When we begin to consider the moral implications within legal decisions, we often find that a specific act and punishment were not incurred for moral reasons, since the intention of the doer is the determiner of its morality, but may be instituted for amoral reasons. These amoral reasons are social objectives which alter the significance of a specific case and may require of an individual retribution for which close inspection will not make him personally guilty, but socially delinquent. Thus, the system of reward and punishment on the human level, which we usually so naturally tend to believe must follow as a consequence of the act's performance or malformance, is not really a consequence thereof. The legal process judges the act and awards punishment and these are each part of its duties. But they are, in the end, separate acts each of which is based on different, although not mutually different, principles.

We have thus digressed to inject a few thoughts on rewards for an act to show that it is not necessary to think of an act in relation to its consequences for one to commit or abstain from committing that act. It is not that people will never consider the consequences. Many people are quite aware of them and would not follow a prescribed action if they were unaware of the consequences thereof. In the sphere of religion, most people act in this fashion. Some would contend that this is the only ace in the hole to maintain religion at all. Perhaps so. But it is based upon a nebulous assumption and an egoistical intention. We must assume the principle of Antignos. Man must work in the vineyard of the L-rd, with the feeling that it is an obligation on his part to do so. There is no purpose necessary and no reward expected. Such is the worker who works for his master with no expectation of rewards. He is born not by his own will, and shall depart not of his own will. In the twain he has no choice but to live. And to exist is to comprehend and express the deeply bound and circumscribed position of man. Not bound by nature, which he can rise above and regulate. But bound within the limits of the Master, which were for him ascribed. For this reason he gives of himself to the Divine. And his services attain the heights of the sacrifice of the total self.

* * *

Thus we have traced the concept of the sacrifice from its initial inception to its final all-inclusive expression. Every type of service to the L-rd is a sacrifice; we are giving of ourselves to the end which is not within ourselves. It is only whether this sacrifice assumes one of two different methods, which we must ascertain. The one is the sacrifice of Cain, which sought to gain a reward for the service rendered. The other was the sacrifice of Abel, who did his service as an obligation upon himself, and with no reward expected. This is also the sacrifice which Isaac was brought up for. I wish you to note here the contrast between this act and its purpose and the similar event which commenced the Christian faiths, the crucifixion. In both events a sacrifice of the life was offered. In the first there is no purpose stated. It is not expected that this event should aid in the uprightness or salvation of future generations. There is no purpose stated to those who were involved in the act or to their future adherents. Not so the Christian act of sacrifice. No Christian can comprehend that event without reference to its purpose or necessity as a means to the salvation of their souls. If that purpose were not to exist in their theological explanations, then they could not accept the event of the crucifixion. This is a point of primary departure between the Jewish and Christian religions. It is perhaps this close identification in the Christian society of salvation with sacrifice which has lead to the disintegration of the entire concept of sacrifice in the modern social system. When this close causal connection is maintained then it is possible for man to state that he dispenses with salvation and dispenses with sacrifice.

Whatever the Christian attitude to sacrifice is, it is only for us to note in contrast to the Jewish concept. This may be a quite difficult concept to grasp and an even more difficult one to live with. It is not my contention that such a concept is the most natural of things for the human being to accept. We are in the main, teleological animals, and are unsatisfied if we cannot depict a specific purpose or cause to an event. But we are also a religious, human race, who do many things for no strict or understandable purpose. And if so many of our logical, purposeful acts can lead to so many man-made evils, we should not feel so uncomfortable at executing acts at times without purpose or full account.

CHAPTER VIII

ISRAEL

In the course of many centuries the term Israel has become the most distinct appellation of the Jews. This name is significant not only for its almost universal institution among Jews, but for a very special concept which it engenders; a concept which is part of the Jewish conceptual scheme. It may be difficult to divorce one's thoughts concerning this term from events which have occurred in the new Jewish commonwealth which bears this name. We should, however, attempt to disengage our thoughts from the very narrow focal point of the State of Israel to the broader focus of the history of Israel. Within that path of history, a unique pattern has been established by Israel.

Before we can proceed further, we must come to grips with a topic which is very prevalent and at the same time always yields ambivalent attitudes. This topic, for lack of any more suitable terminology, I shall identify as "chosenness."

We are all no doubt quite familiar with the epithet of the Jewish nation as the "chosen people." There is little uncertainty that there are present many persons who feel that the very fact that they are, what is called "chosen" makes them necessarily "superior" in some fashion. This valuation of their personalities in terms of their own situation is a false deduction. It is not that the individual or the society is superior in any measurable quantity that it is chosen for a specific task. Furthermore we shall demonstrate that the fact of being a chosen people is not a reward nor a valuation, but entails a specific and often difficult obligation. It is a result of the specific historical fulfillment of the tasks of life which preceded the attainment of the title "the chosen people," that it was applied. And it was rendered only to identify the nation which will continue in the future to fulfill a specific type of social obligation. Far from being a means to establish a select sect, it is another one of those burdens which has been accepted by the Jews.

* * *

The three fathers of Judaism and of Israel, Abraham, Isaac, and Jacob, each contributed paradigms on the best methods to live a complete life in this world. Although they each lived and practiced their ideals to a great extent in a similar fashion, the great performance of Abraham being that he could perpetuate his ideals on to his children, nevertheless each one of the patriarchs represents a special orientation to the problems of life and their fulfillment within a religious framework. After a fashion, these special attitudes of each one towards the best method of religious actions were contrary to each other and could not all be fully accepted. The method which has gained almost universal acceptance among the Jews, although they rarely realize it and even more rarely know how to identify it, is the one which was evolved and championed by Jacob. It is he who proves to have found the most appropriate religious orientation. His life and his actions have left the greatest examples for the Jewish people to follow. It is to his history that we assign most import and profoundest significance.

It would be difficult to ascertain the exact personality characteristics of these three patriarchs. Even generalized attitudes are difficult to extract from the Biblical accounts of their lives. But extract, to the best of our abilities, we must. We can say briefly that Abraham's religious attitude was the one which most involved himself with his neighbors. Perhaps being an initiator caused him to seek adherers from among his fellows in order to more permanently establish the existence of his ideas. His method of neighborly relationships could be called the "open door" policy. He would establish his household always at a strategic spot in the center of town or at an important crossroads and would have his doors open to all passers by. To all who came past he offered solace, bread and rest. He is the paradigm in Jewish history on the fulfillment of the commandment to take into one's household travelers and give them support. All those who came to rest from their journeys would in the course of conversations with their host be told of the ideas which were his cornerstones in life, and some of those who heard were impressed sufficiently to become adherers to his creeds.

In contrast to the very intimate relations Abraham enjoyed with his neighbors, Isaac lived in practical seclusion. He had as little relations with his neighbors as it was at all possible for a household to maintain. He was the absolute sacrifice all during his life which he had been at that one moment on Moriah. He gave his entire life and activities over to adherence to the one and only L-rd. His life was little known to the inhabitants about him, and he was just as unaware of things surrounding him. This was as true of his early life as it was later in life when he lost the use of his eyes. It is due to this mystical detachment from all of life that Isaac was not aware of the true natures of his twin sons. He hardly knew them at all; his only means to recognition of the one over the other being the great hairiness of the elder in relation to the younger son. It was only after the inadvertent, in relation to Isaac, blessing of the younger son Jacob and the violent reactions this caused in Esau, that Isaac became for the first time aware of the true value of each one of his sons. In all of the necessary relations with one's neighbors that were forced upon Isaac, we behold the strict, almost identical following in the patterns which his father had established. Nowhere does he innovate; he uses the methods which were used before him. He is not interested in these outside areas, and the methods used by his father are to him sufficient. So much so that when a hunger season hits Canaan in his own time as it did in his father's, he has to be Divinely instructed not to leave Canaan and go to Egypt as his father had done. (The reason for this admonition is not understood by me, and is in no way here pertinent.) Thus lived Isaac all of his one hundred and eighty years. He gave himself over to the L-rd.

* * *

With these short resume of the lives of Abraham and Isaac, we may proceed to analyze the particular mode of life which Jacob assumed.

Jacob commenced early in life to reassess the means of living which a man may choose. "And the lads grew up and Esau became a hunter, a man who knows the fields, while Jacob remained a dweller in tents, an *ish tam*." The translation of *ish tam* has often been, a "plain man." I feel this is false, and I will translate, as Onkelos before me has done, these words to mean a "complete man." What is herein stated about Jacob? He remained at home during his maturing years in order to gain, in our parlance, an education. He wanted to become a complete person, a man who would contain within himself enough understanding in order to be able to live a human life.

We must now attempt to outline Jacob's ideal for accommodation with his neighbors. This outline will be purely abstract, the proof coming first later as we apply the concept to understanding various parts of the Biblical accounts of Jacob's life.

Jacob spent a great part of his life in the "study hall." He worked many years at learning and at gaining an understanding in every field of scholarship available to him. All this work was not just part of the inquisitive soul which belongs to man. It was a far deeper and more concentrated task. Jacob sought to develop within his personality and his actions that perfection of righteousness and humaneness which would stand out to whoever beheld it. Jacob, in a way, was attempting perhaps to combine the ideals of both of his immediate predecessors into one. He was interested in his neighbors and did not wish to abandon himself to the world as Isaac had done. Neither was he convinced that the best interests of religion are served through the establishment of means of overly direct exchange with his neighbors, as was Abraham's practice. Perhaps he felt this could well lead to an integration of foreign elements into his religious ideals, just as easily as it can spread its own doctrines. The flow of ideas certainly can go both ways; especially if one is not well versed in the values of his own concepts, and has not the means of evaluating other people's ideals. As a long range institution for Judaism, Abraham's method would not suffice, however successful it was when utilized by Abraham. Jacob searched many years for the solution of this problem of finding an adequate means of dealing with one's neighbors. One can never know when he finally arrived at the solution which he finally chose. It seems quite certain that he had the concept for a long time before he was sure of accepting it. He was even uncertain that it was pleasing in the eyes of the L-rd, as we shall illustrate shortly. It perhaps just grew on him more and more and he became intrigued with it. But his reservations concerning it were not easily dispelled. It did somehow smack of compromise. It did not seem on first observation to be as great an orientation to religion as either Abraham's or Isaac's religious mode was. It precipitated much mental undulation on the part of the instigator of this method before he himself was at all sure of its value. All during this long and tedeous mental and spiritual bout, Jacob prepared himself, nevertheless, to be able to carry out his plan. For, above all things else, this religious mode requires of the individual much preparation and building up of stamina. This is what is meant by Jacob being an *ish tam*, a dweller in tents. He spent the great part of his time in the tents in order to become a complete individual. He sought to create a great perfection in his actions. What was his objective? His objective was to be a living, primary example of the way life should be properly conducted. He was interested that people should learn from his ways not by direct instigation, but by indirect emulation. His concept was that if he could learn to lead a correct and just life to a great extent, he would then find respect and adoration for such a life in his neighbors. They would be attracted to his type of life by witnessing the fine qualities thereof, as he practiced it. This would then bring to him people who would know why they like the religion and would have become convinced out of their own volition and through no ulterior pressure. Thus he had to make of himself a paradigm of holiness in the human being. Thus he had to lead a life which was unusual and apart from the general crowd of people and yet would attract some of them as bees are brought to honey. For this he strived so long and for so many years. To perfect his nature and his actions so as to always show the goodness and the righteousness which is possible in any action. Wherever he should sojourn, he would be recognized as that pious individual who it is so wonderful to attempt to imitate. He had his reservations about the fulfillment of this ideal, which is quite understandable. Who can measure whether he is really fulfilling a religious task or a personal passion? Who can guarantee that it will at all be a method worthy of attention to other people? Lastly, who can justify this approach above those which were utilized by Abraham and Isaac? The questions notwithstanding, Jacob embarked with a strong resolution to fulfill his life's task.

* * *

Jacob was forced to flee Canaan and was sent by his parents to *Padan Aram*, the home of Jacob's maternal family. On the way he was necessitated to bed upon a rock, and there had his famous prophecy-dream. We are not here concerned with the interpretation of this event. We only mention it to observe that at this occasion Jacob was given the inheritance of Abraham's blessings. It was to be through Jacob, by way of Isaac, that the L-rd's promises to Abraham were to be realized.

Jacob arose from this perception with very mixed feelings. He felt the great importance of the words which were spoken to him, but he was not quite satisfied. His reaction to this event is very different from that of his forefathers to similar events.

"And he said, now the L-rd is present in this spot and I was unaware of it. And he was terrified and he stated, 'how fearful this place is; this certainly is a dwelling of the L-rd and a heavenly gate.'"

"Then Jacob made a vow, saying thusly, 'If the L-rd will be with me and will protect me on this journey that I am making; and will give me some bread to eat and a cloak to wear; and I will also return to my father's home in peace and the L-rd will remain my G-d, then this stone that I have placed as a marking-stone will mark this place as a Divine home; and of all that is given to me will I give a tithe to You.'"

Let us survey these few Biblical sentences. Several questions will come to mind upon reflection of these passages. It is necessary to understand why Jacob felt terrified at the realization that his dream was not an ordinary one. It is necessary to see the value of Jacob's affirmation that this place is a Divine area. This seems quite unnecessary for us to be told about. What is perhaps of greatest perplexity is why did Jacob make a vow to the L-rd? His requests for some sustenance seem to be quite superfluous coming immediately after the L-rd had promised to him that, "I will protect you and return you to this land, and in no way abandon you until I have fulfilled all that I have told you." These promises were much more then Jacob asks for in his vow, and would preclude anything that Jacob might desire.

We can only understand this sequence of actions by Jacob in the light of that what was most upon his conscience. The L-rd had made him responsible to follow in the footsteps of Abraham and Isaac by giving to him the inheritance of the original promises to Abraham. This placed grave doubts in Jacob as to the ability he would now have to maintain his own fashion for fulfillment of his religious axioms. He felt that there was perhaps a chance that his method of acting as a "living example" would be repudiated by the Divine. There was no reference to his ideas in the prophecy-dream, and this made him even more fearful. He wished to find a positive indication of the value of his judgement, and none was forthcoming. Thus he remarked, since this must be a Divine home and a gateway to heaven, I will take upon myself to seek some affirmation right here for my perplexed and reserved cause. This being the case, he resolved to bid for Divine assistance in fulfilling his aims. That which had been promised to him was that his children would achieve the goal of nationhood and the receiving of this land. He was also promised personal protection and return to the land. He asked in his vow, not for less, but for something additional. He wished to receive assistance on "this specific journey" which I am embarking upon. It was not just the physical journey that he was traveling on that he sought aid for, but for the spiritual journey that he had undertaken as well. He wanted to be given strength enough and protection substantial to allow him to succeed through all the many hazards that would face him in his way of life. He asked to be given only bread and clothing enough to exist. He asked above all to be able to fulfill his goal and remain "at peace with his father" when he returns, and remain true to the Divine. In short, he asked for just enough personal needs to allow him to practice the concept of the "paradigm case" of religion from which his neighbors could seek to emulate, if they so desired. Jacob was undertaking much more then Abraham or Isaac had assumed, and his vow is testimony to the complications which he foresaw concerning his ideal. The promises of the L-rd were essentially for the future and would not in any way aid his accomplishment of his aims. Only if the few desires which he requested in his vow could be vouchsafed to him, would he be more tranquil concerning the encompassing of the task with his limited abilities.

* * *

Many years passed and Jacob lived the life of the "example in piety." Yet his life was ever a series of crises and amid all his concerns stood the perplexity of the worth of his chosen path. The passage of time brought to Jacob the great turning point in his life with his return to Canaan. He had now fled with his family from his father-in-law and presently stood on the threshold of again facing his brother Esau. And again Jacob was overcome with a huge sense of fear. This time his fear was a double one; a concern for the spiritual path that he led and for the physical well-being of his family. And he was much concerned least his troubles were a result of his chosen religious path. And he explained his position in his entreaty to the Divine.

"And Jacob spoke, 'G-d of my father Abraham, and G-d of my father Isaac, L-rd, who told me to return to my land and birthplace, and there I will deal kindly with you. I have become diminished from all the kindness and all the righteousness that you have done with Your servant; for I crossed this Jordan with but a stick, and now have become into twin camps.'" The result of all the favors which you have showered upon me is that my principle has become diminished in its possibility of attainment. What have I as a result of all of these wares that fill up two camps? I have people running after me and waiting before me in order to entrap me. I, who wished to be left alone, to be witnessed from afar, am the object of people's envy and greed. I, who desired that people should seek after my deeds, am the victim of them seeking after my possessions. What for did I need all of these possessions? All I desired in a material way was a small amount of bread and clothing. My own ideal for acting as an object lesson for emulation has become almost defaulted. But I would not complain if this were all. For not only has my own plan been unsuccessful, but the crude Esau has been most successful and stands before me ready to slay all in obligation to his passions. "Save me I beseech of You, from the hands of my brother Esau, for I fear him and that he will come and slaughter mother and child." The result of all my work and the result of all the possessions that I have is that I should be a living prey for the human beasts of the world. I am completely unarmed, physically and spiritually. My method is to show kindness and goodness. This is what I have learned to accomplish to perfection within my character. Such an ability leaves me defenseless against the evil reactions of man towards me. Thus I beg of You to protect me in my defenseless position.

"And Jacob remained alone, and a man wrestled with him until the break of dawn. And he perceived that he could not conquer him, and he touched him upon his thigh, and Jacob's thigh was bruised from struggling with him." Now Jacob was to receive the long awaited verdict on the value of his cause. He had to fight a spiritual battle that night which simulated his spiritual battle with Laban and with Esau. And in that battle he was to learn that his fears were unwarranted. His consternation lest his position be a defenseless one and leave him weak in the face of the evil drives in mankind were unfounded. For in truth his position was mighty and well fortified. Righteousness and piety build around themselves an impregnable wall to protect their host. It is only in the peripheral, in the material that some damage may be incurred in the struggle that may ensue from your ways. It is only in the diminished functioning of a limp that evil may succeed, but not in defeating you and your aims. No, your goal can be and has been a successful one and you have nought to fear from Esau. "And he stated, it should no longer be said your name is Jacob, but it shall be Israel, for you have struggled with G-d and with men, and you have prevailed." You have struggled against the ways man seek to live on this earth and to establish a new pattern by placing yourself as an illustration for others to copy. You have also struggled with the L-rd in that you have forged out a religious pattern which was not given to you by your fathers, nor revealed to you by your L-rd. And it has been a correct method of religious action and you have prevailed in its correctness.

And thus we see that the meeting of Jacob and Esau is a joyous and uneventful one. We see that Esau has gained great respect for his brother and honors him. It is because the wholehearted devotion to goodness and to exemplifying the life of piety which Jacob assumed does appeal even to the most evil-minded of men. They become chastened before the strength of the humaneness in the Israel character. And after they have become weakened in their own methods, they pause to watch the life of goodness, covet it and attempt to duplicate it.

It was for this trait that Jacob was renamed Israel. And it is for this trait that the Jews are called Israel. We are not the biggest among nations, nor are we the mightiest among peoples. It is not because we are better then others that we have been called chosen. It is because we have chosen to act as examples to the world that we have been called an *am segulah*. So it is specifically stated just prior to the giving of the ten commandments.

"You have witnessed what I have done to Egypt, and I have lifted you as on the wings of eagles and brought you to me. And now *if* you will hear my voice, and heed my covenant, then you will be a select group from all the nations unto me, for to me belongs the entire universe. And you should be to me a priestly nation and a holy folk; these words you (Moses) shall deliver to the children of Israel."

The full concept of Jacob is incorporated into the demands of Judaism. It is not enough that you shall act in accordance to the ways taught to you. You must act so well as to make yourselves conspicuous to the nations and they should feel that you are a holy nation. You should perfect yourselves as individuals and as a nation, so that the world will have a paradigm of religious life which it can imitate. It is the culmination of this trait which will cause you to be called a "chosen" people.

* * *

A tribute to the "heritage of Jacob" to Judaism was presented to us by Balaam, whose task for Balak was quite of another nature.

In the midst of the desert, with all its inherent unstable social patterns, the Jews had managed to establish a social order that caused Balaam to exclaim in heights of poetic rhetoric, the beauty of the system. "For I perceive them from the tips of the peaks, and from the heights I view them; lo, they are a nation who dwells apart, and do not count themselves among the peoples! Who would count the sands of Jacob, and measure the offspring of Israel; may I be worthy of a righteous one's death and would that my final shall be as his." Balaam stands over a projecting height and with his accompaniment takes sight of the camp

146

of the Israelites on the desert floor below. And in astonished tones he portrays his feelings. I not only physically, but intellectually stand from a propitious vantage point and thus can comprehend the nation which is encamped beneath us. It is truly a nation that dwells separate from all other nations. It does not at all reckon itself according to the values used by others. It has so much of value within itself that it need not be envious of other folks. Who would be so erroneous as to attempt to evaluate this nation by counting it; who could be so callous as to judge this nation as insignificant by measuring the total of its offspring. However small in numbers it may be, would that my death should occur while I were part of them; would that I were able to gain an end similar to that which they are privileged to possess.

And why is it that Balaam should so covet to be part of Israel? It is since Balaam beheld the purity and the freshness of the Israelite nation. "And he, Balaam, lifted his words in parable and said . . . How glorious are the tents of Jacob, the dwellings of Israel. They are as the cool stretching brooks, as the gardens which hang against the river; as the aromatic plants which the L-rd has planted, as the cedars which line the waters." This is the scene which Balaam beheld in the very midst of the hot, thirsty desert. He found a people who enticed him with their wonderful purity of social existence. He felt the extreme purity of the nation of escaped slaves to esteem it in the parable of the beauty of brook, of the coolness of the glen, of the colorfulness of the gardens, of the quiet might of the cedars. I don't think that the vision of Israel was ever more pleasantly or more dramatically portrayed then it was by the evil seer of the desert.

* * *

The existence of the Jewish people over an era of over fifteen hundred years in utter dispersement and through terrible deprivations is one of the mysteries of the world. It would be a pleasant mystery if it were not for the awful but very apparent fact that many has been the time that Jewish persecution has been a result of violent reactions to the incomprehensibility of our neighbors of this mystery. All sorts of truncated reasoning has crept into the ideas of one nation after the other in their viewing of the Jews, and as often-times referred to, the Jewish problem. Little or no means have been at our disposal to enable us to belie many of the accusations and castigations which have followed the Jew across the face of the earth. The many diversified demands which have been placed upon the Jews bear witness to the fact that the existence of this people has been incongruous to the nations, but in no distinct discernible fashion.

I wish that it were within my power to lift the mystery from off the shoulders of our existence. If this were at all possible, I feel that it would have been accomplished long ago. The mystery stems not from the mere fact of existence, but from the manner of maintenance of the dispersed segments of the nation. And that manner of maintenance is, in the final analysis, based upon those two unique modes de vivre which I have outlined in these last two chapters. These two concepts which are so intertwined into the fabric of Jewish living that one has difficulty in extracting and examining them, are at the core of the mysteriousness of the facts of the Jewish existence. They are concepts which are not dominant in other similar spheres of activity. Moreover they are concepts which largely tend to isolate the mainstream of the Jewish social existence away from that of their immediate neighbors. We have already contrasted the Jewish sacrifice concept with that which prevails in

148

Christianity. Similarly the method of internal reformation and personal reconstruction is very incomprehensible to a world which is dominated with the idea of mission work to one's neighbors. In all the years of its existence, only once was Judaism fated to partake in a type of missionary recruitment, and this event was rather an ill-fated event in the perspective of history. We have not needed this sort of weapon to make us mighty, or numerous; certainly it was unnecessary for our survival. Within this concept is integrated the thought which Balaam saw so vividly from his perch atop a mountain. The Jews can fulfill their "role in history" only by living apart from their neighbors and as a small insignificant people whose chief raison d'etre is to be an object of curiosity by their more numerous neighbors. But one has the hope that these indirect methods will prove to be effectual in causing a rapprochement of Judaism with its neighbors. This can be accomplished not by any compromise of the Jewish concepts of life, as many are wishing to do, but by the realization that Judaism and the Jews represent a vehicle for the emergence of the submerged spiritual humanity of the world today.

EPILOGUE

We have traversed a labyrinth of ideas since we first left the confines of our inner mind and ventured to think in writing. Perhaps to many this work might be more conspicuous by what it has failed to deal with than with what it has much belabored. It has not been my intention to discuss theology and if my work is labeled as within the boundaries of theology, I would be grievously hurt. None of the topics which are most dear to theological discussion have found their way into our work. One must look very long indeed to find any mention of such topics as the afterworld, theism, and ceremonial organization; all the perennial stock in trade of all theological discussion. Our discussion, I should like to feel, has taken as its point of departure a step past these topics.

Of course it will disturb some that I have not ventured to herein state that last and most profoundly logical proof of the existence of G-d. In fact I have to the best of my feeble abilities attempted to avoid even the usage of any special appellation of the Deity. If one were to take a poll of the word most often used in America today, I would be very surprised if that word were not the monosyllable word G-d. Perhaps the word *I* would rival it. And this is perhaps the best summation of religion today. There has been a coalescence of the words I—G-d in preponderance of usage and even in measuring of usage. It is in this connection that I avoid using a name for the Divinity to the greatest extent possible. For nothing could be further away to myself then the Being and even the knowledge of G-d. And by avoiding any specific reference to it beyond those inherently involved already in a discussion, I am demonstrating my lack of equipment to delve more intricately into that topic.

It is this close relationship of all existence with the I

—ego of the self that causes men so often to announce that they wish to have a proof of the Divine's existence. This may be unpalatable to some, but I personally am of the opinion that the very nature of our existence limits our ability to give any proof of the Divine existence or even to come in real contact with the Divinity. If one is to offer one of the many substitutes for the true Divinity which are extant, then these could use human vindication. But the Divine itself constitutes something which is a-natural and a-human and as such can neither be comprehended nor contacted. Along with this concept goes my feeling that much of this prevalent business of being "near G-d" or "contacting the L-rd" is much a perversion of religion and of man's role in religion. But the uninitiated will therefore ask, how does one know G-d exists? The answer to that one is quite simple. One does not know unless the Divine chooses to reveal His existence. The world can be maintained quite substantially without knowledge of the Divine existence and certainly the Divine is complete without recourse to our knowledge of Him. We only know of the Divine existence today because it was revealed to us these many thousands of years ago on Moriah in the words "I am your L-rd, G-d." Why the L-rd chose at that time to reveal his presence is neither within my power to explain nor within my wishes to undertake. It is, in the end, as all of the L-rd's creations; His Wish.

With these rebellious statements I leave all theological polemics to those more inclined to deal in them. As for the explanation of ritualia, this is of course an intriguing business. I think that such would be the task of one who wishes to follow up, as it were, the concepts herein enumerated. But for me it is a most unrewarding task. First of all, the task runs into the difficulty of transcending the numerous generations which separate the final product from its inception, and which necessarily alter its complexion. Furthermore, the concepts are not applied individually into a specific rite, but several are therein incorporated. To unlock the various strands which constitute a rite is most difficult. Lastly, I am not convinced that much will be obtained from an adequate and full analysis of any and all ceremonial objects. It is not axiomatic that a sufficient explanation will make a specific rite more readily practicable. Certainly I do not feel that the ideas herein expounded will necessarily in any way convert people into being more Jewish or Jewish conscious. It may prove to be a force in divorcing some who are unwilling to assume of the difficult obligations which are concomitant with my Jewish weltanschauung. We are beings who seek explanation for things which occur and also for items which we negotiate. But the explanation will not in any fashion determine our acceptance or rejection of a specific mode. Usually it is our prior acceptance or rejection of a mode which will cause us to find favor or otherwise with a given explanation thereof.

* * *

Now we should attempt a short restatement of the principal ideas that we have sought herein to express.

We commenced this task on a very rigid logical plain. It was our investigation into the processes of the world and of the human being which led us to find a most uncomfortable and incomprehensible facet to our presence in the universe. The world was created to remain a viable entity only when it could maintain stabilization. It is so constituted that it is in any analysis a product of twin actions which are complementary and function to the opposite ends in each change which is in the system incurred. Each action which is incurred calls forth a simultaneous reaction which acts to nullify the import of the action. Man has quite another "system" upon which he chooses to function. Inherently his constitution seeks for an ever greater increase in the universe. This is a result of the salient facet of man's composition, his need to create. He is most concerned with the imposition of a permanent signature to the universe and with an ever expanding existence due to his own invention. He is quite displeased to learn that all of his efforts may be very illusory in a universe which extracts a like return for every step which is taken forward. An impasse between the realms of nature and of man is reached. It has been our contention that this impasse is only so as a result of man's attempt to utilize his facilities to create within the boundaries of nature. When this is so, he is responsible for the consequences which ensue from such a policy. The results are great natural reactions which compensate for any gains sought. The paradigm of this is the saga of Egypt. The result of the great physical upsurge of the civilization was a concomitant enslavement of the great masses of people of the nation. No other method would have sufficed to maintain a social equilibrium under those heavy construction schedules.

Man was not given life in order to enslave or become enslaved. The social order of Egypt had to be destroyed and one more in harmony with man's inner construction had to be devised. Whether man could have accomplished this all alone is not for us to give final statement about. History is studded with many failures and we are having difficulty in discovering any successes. The presentation of a social order which would have a stability and would yet be able to maintain its creative energies was the significance of Mount Sinai. We have shown that the numerous and interconnected precepts concerning idolatry are all admonishments concerning the interaction man should have with his perceivable environment. It has been our contention that the concepts of Tumah and Sabbath are closely intertwined with our problem of adjustment in the universe. They are not mere creations of vacuum or of unstable psychological tranquilizers in the social order. They are concerned with the attaining of the possibility of creation in the universe on the part of the individual. Tumah is concerned with diminishing the need and the amount of participation in only physical reality in order to have man spend some of his efforts within the spiritual reality with which he is born. The Sabbath is the establishing of a specific time and a specific life mode which will be conducive to working with man's creative abilities.

Superimposed upon these fundamental concepts and permeating them in all of their manifestations are the twin concepts of Olah; the complete sacrifice of oneself, and Israel; the prime example of conduct. These two concepts, in their ideology and in their intensity, are unique to the Jewish religion. They complement each other and add that special burden of responsibility which is apparent when one views the Jewish social order. They also are accountable for that very mysterious external with which one perceives the Jew. It is not an accident or a willful perversion of the image of a Jew which has led to his being viewed as separate and unfathomable. This is the theory of those who are very familiar with Jews and Judaism and cannot deem it possible that they should be ill-conceivable to the mass of gentile people. Yet I think that aside from considerations of socio-dynamics which will place the Jews in the general category of minorities (and therefore subject to the many adverse occurrences and allegations which are part of the price for a minority's seeking to fight acculturation) the Jews are always seen by their neighbors as something quite unusual and different from any other minority.

It is this inexplicable difference about the Jews which has led to so many disastrous consequences. And I attribute this entire phenomenon to the mechanics of maintaining a nation which is in reality very much interested in its neighbors and yet pretending to be busy only in its own vineyard. This is exactly the result of seeking to influence the world by the indirect method which was the chosen path of Jacob. Perhaps the greatest tragedy is that we ourselves are so completely unaware of the true nature of our existence that we can in no intelligible fashion defend ourselves from violent onslaughts or terrible accusations. I think that the first step towards some control of our destiny is our recognition of the strange view which the outside world receives of the Jew. This is aside from the value which we obtain from self knowledge in aiding us to live in the confines of Judaism and in evaluating the various trends and actions which claim their appropriateness in the name of Judaism.

* * *

Now we must close the circle by returning to the opening items of this work. We had stated that a primary motivating factor causing us to divulge these concepts into the public eye was the very fashion which religion today enjoys in America. We are well aware of the numerical increase in the so categorized church-going population. There are not a few among the religious leaders of these United States who feel that this portrays an ever heightening trend towards the re-establishment of the religious institution to high value among Americans. This statement is at once both true and false. It is true if one is willing to only evaluate religion by the quantity of its adherents. When we delve into the quality of the religious participation of Americans, it would be difficult to arrive at a very optimistic prognosis. It cannot be stated that the great majority of people who utilize religious institutions do so with a religious intent. It cannot be truly within the realm of possibility to rationalize every card party, dance, and discussion group as a religious act. It is very doubtful religious value that we can ascribe to gymnastics, home grown philosophy, one legged psychological tranquilizing discussions, and Saturday night bingo games; all favorite activities of today's community religious center. Those religious leaders who present the thesis that these and similar activities lead to a new religious awareness are only fooling themselves. This sort of community entertainment, which is at once very pleasurable and by its wide acceptance and religious approval always "clean" and praise-worthy, serves a definite socio-psychological fulfillment value. We do not add to its value one iota by attaching a vestigial appendage to it, the religious institution. This does, through parasitic methods, help to maintain the religious institution; we would perhaps have discarded many of them a long time ago had they not built a multi-million dollar "social center." To a greater degree than even in legitimate advertising, the sponsor is entirely divorced from the product. No amount of advantage can be discerned in a basketball game played in the community church over a similar one held in a nonsectarian or public community center.

Even the individuals who attend their religious institution for religious purposes do so for quite a different religious reason than the one advocated by religious leaders. I think that it can be safely stated that any religious concept which is today maintained, and one is here alluding to real religious concepts and not to pseudo-religious social motives of society, is radically altered from those of which they are derived, in the great majority of instances. We often use the same vocabulary and phraseology which our forefathers used, but we invariably mean something different when we use them than what was meant by them to generations who preceded us. It is not my intention to attempt to document this statement. I leave it for others to either verify or disapprove. But I think that most people will concur with this statement and will also agree that the very great and fundamental upheavals which our century has wrought are in great measure responsible for the altered religious conceptualization of mankind today. Can we diagnose this shift in religious ideology? I don't really know if we could. I myself certainly feel quite incapable of doing so at present. At best I could only allude to some of the symptoms of the changed religious atmosphere. I feel that the most manifest of symptoms of the new religious ideology is that it is at once very greatly desanctified and very greatly abstracted from the common denominator of social activity. These two aspects are opposites, perhaps compensatory developments of each other. By desanctification of religion I refer primarily to those scenes in religious conduct to which I have already given some space. There has occurred a watering down of religious life so that in its general depiction on the American scene, the mass religious movements, religious and secular are not at all demarcated. We must recognize any special religious function through the association of some symbolic regalia or paraphernalia. The small substream of religious activity which is very "orthodox" in its adherence to religious functions is usually quite devout and intense in its emotional religious involvement, quite correctly recognizes and castigates the majority religious activity as pseudo and shallow, and has become divorced from the principal activities of society. Its practices are in themselves disconnected from the majority of the population and from the majority of the individual's regular activities. This completely unrelated activity to the activities of daily living has only marked religion in its extreme mystical sects. The great currents of religion have been very close to the activities of man and have been integrated with his daily cares and desires. This integration has been close but yet apart. It has touched man in his entire livelihood but brought a new, uncommon and sanctified spirit to it. This classical religion is certainly very rarely witnessed in the neo-religious activity on the modern scene.

* * *

Religion, in all of its diversified manifestations has had to wrangle with two problems throughout most of recorded history. The first problem is the purely theological question of the relationships of the Supreme Authority to the Universe in general and to man in particular. This is a problem which we only brushed past as we went along on our own interests. In the long run, this problem has been usually resolved in what I describe as binding the L-rd to the particular wishes of man. As I am very acutely aware of this failure on man's part and am less than willing to commit such an error myself, I shied away from this religious perplexity. A second problem of religion has been the relationship of one religion to that of another or all others. This problem concerns the validity of religious claims for which each seek ultimate recognition and which cannot all be accepted at the same time. I would venture to state that this problem is not any nearer today towards solution than the first one which we presented.

To these two burdensome perplexities, ones which have so often caused very reasonable men to abandon all ties with organized religion, has been added a third complexity. This is a burden which gnaws much closer to the foundation of religion than the other two. This problem is the justification of religion as a whole in the modern world. We have achieved so many varied tangible material advances in other fields that the religious institution has been found by many to be functionless. The large amount of watered down practices, parasitic attachment to other social activities, bombastic exhortations, and dime-store pamphleteering on such topics as "How to be a good Jewish papa in five easy lessons" will not salvage an institution whose foundations have become shaken. We may be very correct and state that it is wrong for modern people to ask that religion fulfill a purpose, however specific and however small. Yet we live in a very pragmatic era and we cannot readily change such a basic value premise of our society. In order to justify the one towards the other we should twist neither one. A perversion remains a perversion, no matter how much we sugarcoat the result. No matter how great our sentimentality for an old friend such as religion may be, we would only do her an injustice if we were to sustain her on the basis of distorted premises and half baked reasoning.

This work has been dealing with this last problem. If there has been any real purpose in this work, this has been to attempt to realign the thinking of those who care to think concerning religion. Perhaps it would be right to say that I have attempted to write unfashionably on a very fashionable subject. Towards this, I have given a conception of life which is extant, which can be a purpose for religious activity. I have taken the liberty to commence a rapprochement between modern society and its interests and needs with the institutions of my own religion. This work is in no way to be construed as more than a modest commencing of what may prove to be a very long and difficult task. I do not think that the approach which I have chosen to assume is the only one available or the only one possible. Yet I do have hopes that it may suffice in being

159

at least an adequate approach to religion. But evaluation of ideas is a privilege for others than an author to assume.

Religion has enormous functions to perform in those two areas where she has traditionally been of greatest value. The first is the sustenance of the individual vis-a-vis society. Often the individual becomes submerged under the heavy demands and prestige of society. Religion has been the giver of courage and importance to each individual, no matter what station in social life. Religion also has the task of seeing that the over-abundant energies and qualities of man are utilized and not frustrated. Here indeed is a very important task. The most neglected of commodities are the powers of the human psyche. Even in societies where the whole being is not almost entirely used to sustain life itself, it is usually spent quite freely on frivolity. It is religion and its activities which can give to man a Lebens-anschauung which will cause him to lead a valuable and self-fulfilling life.

In conclusion we can state the saying of Rabbi Tarfon in Abot. "Rabbi Tarfon was wont to say: The day is short and the work is exceedingly heavy, but the workers are slothful while the reward is great, and above all the land-lord crowds (for results)." And what results are expected? The goal, which we ourselves cannot know when it is completed under our present circumstances, is; "And it will be that the L-rd will be recognized as King over the entire Universe, on that day the L-rd will be Unity and His name shall be One."